The Gospel of César Chávez

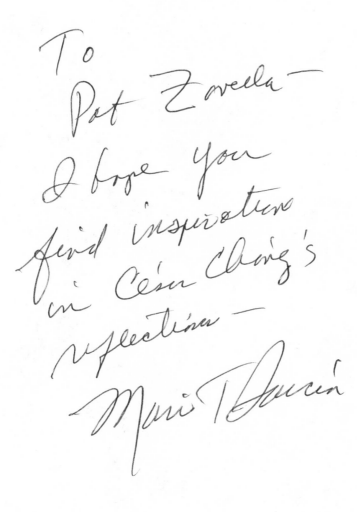

To
Pat Zavella —
I hope you
find inspiration
in César Chávez's
reflections —

Mario T. García

The Gospel of César Chávez

My Faith in Action

Edited and Introduced by
Mario T. García

SHEED & WARD
Lanham • Chicago • New York • Toronto • Plymouth, UK

Permission has been obtained to use quotes from Jacques Henry Levy,
Cesar Chavez: Autobiography of La Causa, Norton cloth edition, © 1975,
University of Minnesota paperback edition © 2007

Published by Sheed & Ward
An imprint of Rowman & Littlefield Publishers, Inc.
A wholly owned subsidiary of The Rowman & Littlefield Publishing Group, Inc.
4501 Forbes Boulevard, Suite 200
Lanham, MD 20706

Estover Road
Plymouth PL6 7PY
United Kingdom

Distributed by National Book Network

Copyright © 2007 Mario T. García

British Library Cataloguing in Publication Information Available

Library of Congress Cataloging-in-Publication Data

García, Mario T.
   The gospel of César Chávez : my faith in action / Mario T. García.
      p. cm. — (Celebrating faith)
   Includes bibliographical references.
   ISBN-13: 978-1-58051-223-7 (pbk. : alk. paper)
   ISBN-10: 1-58051-223-2 (pbk. : alk. paper)
   1. Liberation theology. 2. Chavez, Cesar, 1927—Religion. 3. Mexican
Americans—Religion. 4. Latin Americans—Religion. 5. Latin America—
Religious life and customs. I. Title.

BT83.57.G37 2007
230'.2092—dc22   2007010721

Printed in the United States of America

∞™ The paper used in this publication meets the minimum requirements of
American National Standard for Information Sciences—Permanence of Paper
for Printed Library Materials, ANSI/NISO Z39.48-1992.

To Giuliana García and Carlo García,
my daughter and son whom I love so much.
I hope the spirit and example of César Chávez,
whom you met as children,
will inspire you throughout your lives.

~

Contents

Acknowledgments

The inspiration for this book on the spirituality of César Chávez came from my relationship with Father Virgilio Elizondo. In the late 1990s, I arranged to host Fr. Virgilio as a regents lecturer, a distinguished visiting appointment, in the Department of Chicano Studies at the University of California, Santa Barbara (UCSB). I had never met him before, but I knew of his reputation as the leading Latino Catholic theologian in the United States. Fr. Virgilio's successful visit then led to a series of additional visiting appointments at UCSB to initiate courses in Chicano/Latino Catholic studies on our campus. One significant class that he taught was a graduate seminar on contemporary mystics in which he included César Chávez as one. Through sitting in on this seminar and his other classes and marvelous conversations with Fr. Virgilio at so many lunches and dinners as well as visits to my home, I began to think of doing a book on the spirituality of Chávez. Fr. Virgilio's inspiration has led to this book, and I therefore want to thank him first and foremost. I am honored that it is being published in his distinguished series.

I want to thank Monica Sánchez and Colleen Ho, my research assistants, for their help in this project.

Of course, I am grateful for the editorial support and assistance at Sheed & Ward including Jim Langford, John Loudon, Sarah Stanton, and Elaine McGarraugh.

Finally, as always, to Ellen, who shares my ups and downs but is always there with her love and belief in me and who in the 1970s as a graduate student at University of California, San Diego, served as a human billboard in support of the farm workers.

~

Foreword

It is with enthusiastic pleasure that I introduce this marvelous work by Mario García on the spiritual basis of the life of this great icon of sanctity and justice. I dare say that, along with Martin Luther King, we have had none greater in our times. The amazing thing is that César was simply another man from the barrio, so what made him so powerful and successful? Many have known César Chávez as a great labor organizer, but few have known the ultimate basis of his wisdom, courage, vision, and endless energy. Because César allowed the grace and wisdom of God to infiltrate his entire being during his long sessions of prayer and fasting, through many painful and difficult struggles, he was able to bring about miracles on behalf of justice, especially for the poorest and most defenseless of our country—the migrant farm workers and their families.

César took on a task that nobody thought could succeed. Rooted in the religious tradition he had received from his Mexican family, illuminated with the social doctrine of the Catholic Church, inspired by such nonviolent leaders as Gandhi, St. Francis, and Martin Luther King, and empowered with the best tactics of community organizing, he became the contemporary Moses who would lead his people out of slavery on pilgrimage to the promised land, the David who was not afraid to take on Goliath, and the Jesus who would confront Jerusalem for the sake of his people. He was truly a man of God.

The very title of the book might certainly be disconcerting to many Christians as we believe that there is only one gospel, that of Jesus of Galilee, the Christ. Jesus alone is the good news of God's redemption. There are many versions, such as Matthew, Mark, Luke, and John. But all are based on the life and works of one man: Jesus, the Son of Mary, the carpenter from Nazareth, the Son of God. At first reading, I was disturbed by the title. It sounded like Mario García was proposing a new gospel. Yet upon reflection I was fascinated by it. After all, the gospel is best experienced and appreciated when we encounter persons who are truly living it.

I was privileged to know and work with César Chávez. Like Mario and many others of various ethnicities and religions, I too was inspired by him. He was a man of great simplicity and integrity whose very presence radiated the beauty of God's grace and whose words transformed hearts. Filled with the love of God that he had inherited from his parents and the simple expressions of faith practiced by the Mexican people, he was not afraid to denounce the greed of the owners, which dehumanized the farm worker while announcing new possibilities for a better humanity for everyone. He was gentle but fearless, simple but wise, patient but relentless, respectful but forceful.

For César Chávez the gospel of Jesus was not mere beautiful words to be proclaimed, studied, and quoted. For him, the gospel had to become part of one's innermost being so as to become real and effective in today's world. As St. Paul said, "I live now not I, but it is Christ who lives in me" (Galatians 2:20). César allowed Christ to live in him and to act through him. Thus his life is truly the living gospel of Jesus Christ. As the Cursillo movement had taught him, he became the arms, the feet, and the voice of Christ among his people.

We owe a tremendous debt of gratitude to Mario García for allowing the spiritual voice of César Chávez to come directly to us through the pages of this book. This is not a commentary about César, but his own voice coming to us allowing us to share in the spiritual force that animated and directed him. Because he was truly a mystic in communion with the God of love, he could be sensitive to the pains, the cries, and the suffering of people in ways that others ignored. His spiritual life, like that of Jesus, was not an escape from the struggles of life but rather a deeper insertion into the human struggles between the evil forces of this world and the irruption of the reign of unlimited love.

I have no doubt that this book will be a great source of inspiration for all who read it, and more than that it will show the force of Christian spirituality in the transformation of society—truly the power of God unto holiness.

Virgil Elizondo
University of Notre Dame

César Chávez circa 1980s. UCLA Department of Special Collections, Charles E. Young Research Library.

~

Introduction

César Chávez is one of the great figures in the history of the United States in the twentieth century and, I maintain, one of its great spiritual figures. César—as most who knew him simply called him—accomplished what no other U.S. labor leader had been able to do: successfully organize farm workers. Others had tried and had given up, saying that it was almost impossible to unionize these workers because, among other things, they were always migrating and their lack of permanency did not lend itself to organization. Others gave up due to the strong opposition by growers backed by their supporters in government and law enforcement who decried and destroyed any effort to have their workers unionized. Unionization, the growers believed, would deprive them not only of a cheap labor source, but, perhaps even more significant, of a perceived manageable labor force.

César Chávez overcame these obstacles and beginning in 1965 commenced what became the first successful effort to organize and unionize farm workers in California, the country's richest agricultural state with the largest number of farm workers. These mostly Mexican and Filipino workers joined what became the United Farm Workers (UFW). For almost thirty years until his death in 1993, César labored and struggled to support and enhance the working and living conditions of the most

1

oppressed strata of labor in the United States. These "forgotten Americans" enriched and fed the country through their labor, yet reaped little of the fruits of their labor. Treated as second-class citizens, and facing class and racial discrimination, farm workers toiled in what Carey McWilliams in his marvelous texts on California called "Factories in the Fields." In these conditions, farm workers gathered what Edward R. Murrow further called the "Harvest of Shame."

But the historical importance of César Chávez, at the same time, transcends labor history. Indeed, he was seen in his time, and even more so after his death, as a great civil rights leader among Mexican Americans and by extension other Latino groups in the United States. Some even referred to him as the "Chicano Moses" or the "Chicano Messiah." There is no question but that César represents the most recognized Latino figure in U.S. history, as attested by the recent issue of a César Chávez commemorative stamp by the postal service. It was César's struggle and that of the farm workers that stimulated and encouraged what came to be known as the Chicano movement of the 1960s and 1970s, which, on the one hand, expanded a historical struggle by Mexican Americans for civil rights, and, on the other, focused as never before on Mexican Americans asserting what some refer to as "cultural citizenship"—that is, the right to assert pride in one's ethnic and racial heritage in a way that is respected alongside that of other Americans of diverse backgrounds. As an ethnic leader, César has been likened to Dr. Martin Luther King, Jr. Both were giants in their own time and have been elevated to a form of political sainthood.

***

At an even larger level, César, as did Dr. King, stood for a recognition that the work of American democracy was, and still is, not over. In César's time, Mexican Americans and other Latinos were still marginalized and neglected Americans. They represented part of what Michael Harrington in the early 1960s called "The Other America." Not just as farm workers, but as urban workers in industries and services, Mexican Americans were segregated in low-skill jobs, historically referred to as "Mexican jobs" in the Southwest, where historically most Mexican Americans have lived, that paid menial and, in too many cases, unlivable wages that had been historically labeled "Mexican wages." Further segregated in urban barrios with inadequate housing and public facilities, Mexican Americans had to send their children to segregated and inferior so-called "Mexican schools." These were public schools, going back to the early twentieth century, that provided separate but low-level education for Mexican American students who were expected only to reinforce in time the cheap and low-skilled labor force that their parents represented. As such, while Mexican Americans, including many of immigrant background, worked hard and asked for no handouts, they were not integrated into the folds of American democracy. Neither the American dream nor the melting pot touched their lives.

Despite such discrimination, Mexican Americans over the years struggled to obtain full rights as Americans or as permanent residents and to be respected for their backgrounds and traditions. They stood as reminders, although not much heeded, that Mexican Americans were not strangers to the history of the United States. They were historical descendants, in part, of the early Spanish-Mexican settlements in what came to be the Southwest region of the country. It was these ancestors who named the many settlements that much later would become major American cities: El Paso, Albuquerque, Santa Fe, San Antonio, Tucson, San Diego, Los Angeles, Santa Barbara, and San Francisco, to name just a few. Rivers and mountain ranges and deserts also carried this Spanish-Mexican footprint. And so too did the people, many of whom had mixed with the native Indian communities. It was these original inhabitants of the region—El Norte—that were affected by the war between the United States and Mexico in the 1840s, the U.S.-Mexican War (1846–1848). This mid-nineteenth-century expression of U.S. expansionism, referred to as Manifest Destiny, led not only to the military defeat of Mexico, but to the annexation by the United States of Mexico's northern territories and almost half of Mexico itself. Geography followed expansion. El Norte became the Southwest. The war, in turn, created a new American ethnic group: Mexican Americans. Those Mexican who resided in the conquered territories were allocated citizenship—albeit what became second-class citizenship—and found themselves living in a new country although they represented, along with the Indians, the original settlers. Further historical ironies followed. They became regarded as "strangers," as "foreigners," as "the other," and as "immigrants." Yet as later Chicanos would point out, these Mexican Americans had not come to the border; the border had come to them.

The history of Mexican Americans is, in part, shaped by the theme of conquest. As a result, Mexican Americans begin their experience within the United States not as immigrants, the saga of most other Americans with the exception of Indians and enslaved blacks, but as a conquered people. The initial generation of Mexican Americans represents what I call the Conquered Generation in Chicano history, and they experienced what later Chicano historians referred to as "internal colonialism" in what historian Rodolfo Acuña in his classic history of Chicanos called "Occupied America." Undergoing the central trial of a subjugated population, this generation of Mexican Americans faced the impact of U.S. racism and class oppression that resulted in loss of lands, political second-class citizenship, and racial and cultural discrimination.

Limited in numbers (about 100,000 at the conclusion of the U.S.-Mexican War) and dispersed throughout the Southwest, Mexican Americans might well have become only a footnote in U.S. history except for a momentous change. By the turn of the twentieth century, the Southwest became integrated into the new industrial economy of the country. Industrial captains of industry found in the region—the Mexican Cession—valuable industrial ores such as copper to support the industrial process. Moreover, the region could also provide, especially with federally subsidized irrigation projects, much-needed foodstuffs in the form of vegetables and fruit that could help feed the industrial armies being assembled in the East and Midwest, much of this labor source the result of new immigration from eastern and southern Europe—the "new immigrants." While American capital and know-how were instrumental in exploiting these new southwestern sources of much-needed ores and food products, what was lacking was labor. After failing with Asian and European labor due to racism against the Chinese and the abundance of work for European immigrants elsewhere, corporate employers such as the railroads (needed to open up the Southwest for development), mines, agribusiness, and related enterprises turned to Mexico for their labor needs. As a result, thousands of Mexican immigrant workers began to cross the U.S.-Mexico border, in many cases enticed and even contracted by American employers before they crossed. Close to a million Mexican immigrants entered the United States between 1900 and 1930.

This "great migration," in turn, proved to be a microcosm of our later global economy. That is, American investments in Mexican railroads, in mining, and indirectly in commercial agriculture created the so-called push conditions that dislocated thousands of Mexicans and led to their migration across the border. For example, the American investment and construction of railroads in Mexico opened up commercial agriculture that led to the formation of corporate-style farms that forced many peasants off their small land holdings in order to create large-scale production. Many of these peasants along with other Mexicans became the source of mass immigration to the United States. The global or transnational nature of this change in Mexico is evident when one sees that these immigrants were then employed by the same U.S. railroads that had created their dislocation in their home country. The hunger of American employers for the cheap labor represented by these immigrants formed the "pull" that also characterized the origins of mass Mexican immigration to the United States.

Political revolution in Mexico in the form of the Mexican Revolution of 1910, in addition, expanded the push forces that increased the number of Mexican immigrants and refugees that sought haven across the border. The symbols of this revolution led in part by agrarian leaders such as Emiliano Zapata would be rediscovered by César Chávez in his version of a peasant revolution and by the self-styled "revolutionaries" of the Chicano movement.

The initial generation of Mexican immigrants, or what I call the Immigrant Generation in Chicano history, is part of the larger saga of immigration to the United States. However, one of the differences that characterized Mexican immigrants was that rather than crossing vast oceans, they needed to cross only a mostly land border or the shallow Rio Grande River. Having easy access to the United States and welcomed by greedy employers, Mexican immigrants proved to be the backbone for the wealth of the Southwest in the form of new railroad development, agriculture, and mining. Without the Mexican immigrants, despite the stereotypes of the lazy Mexican, the Southwest could not have undergone a rapid and lucrative (for employers) growth. In return, however, Mexican immigrants, as already noted, faced new and enlarged forms of racial and class discrimination and oppression. To be a "Mexican" now on this side of the border was to be considered by too many white Americans to be members of an inferior "race."

Although handicapped by their vulnerable immigrant status and their dreams of returning at some point to Mexico, some Mexican immigrants struggled to be treated fairly and with respect. Sometimes this took the form of labor strikes or joining labor unions. In other cases, immigrants banded together in mutual benefit societies (*mutualistas*) for self-help as well as in other community-based groups. Immigrants stood up for themselves when pushed too far, as is the case today. Still, as immigrants, with or without documents, they felt more intimidated or were more careful not to engage in public protests.

This, however, would not be the same for many of their children, born and raised in the United States and who as U.S. citizens were more cognizant of their rights and clearer on their expectations for opportunities to integrate into American society. As such, this generation of Mexican Americans by the 1930s and beyond forged the first significant although dispersed civil rights movement in Chicano history. I refer to this generation as the Mexican American Generation. Through new leadership that reflected their interests and concerns as U.S. citizens, the Mexican American Generation through groups such as the League of United Latin American Citizens (LULAC) and the American G.I. Forum between the 1930s and the 1960s struggled on a variety of fronts for first-class citizenship for Mexican Americans and against barriers for integration. These struggles included efforts to eliminate school segregation and job, wage, and housing discrimination, as well as to achieve effective political representation, among other issues.

An important aspect of this generation struggle was that thousands of Mexican Americans fought bravely in World War II. It has been estimated that perhaps as many as half a million Mexican Americans and other Latinos participated in the war effort as part of the U.S. military. The "good war" not only socialized them to the goals of the conflict centered on the defense of democracy, but motivated many of them after the war to no longer tolerate anything less than democracy at home. This spurred the civil rights struggles. Some successes were achieved although, for the most part, Mexican Americans at the end of this period continued to face widespread and severe forms of discrimination. What was gained was a sense of empowerment for this generation of activists. Their struggles laid the foundation for the more widespread and aggressive ones of the Chicano movement. It is out of this historical context that the story of César Chávez emerges.

***

César Chévez was born on March 31, 1927, in the San Luis Valley near Yuma, Arizona, the child of hard-working Mexican American small farmers. His parents had both been born in northern Mexico but had lived in the United States for many years. His mother and grandmother, who lived with them, particularly socialized him and his four siblings. It was these devout Catholic women who influenced César to be nonviolent, to care about the welfare of others, and to give to those in need. This socialization laid the foundation for César's profound spirituality. But the family struggled, especially during the Great Depression. Not able to pay his property taxes, César's father saw his farm taken over by the state, and he had to later sell it for very little. César's parents had no choice but to leave Arizona in 1939 with their family and migrate, along with many other Americans, to seek a better fortune in California. In the "golden state," César and his family did not strike it rich. Instead, they joined the army of migrant workers so well captured in the novels of John Steinbeck. Following the crops, the Chávez family lived in one labor camp after another, often with little food and little shelter. One consequence of this migration was that César and his siblings had to have their education constantly interrupted. He recalls attending thirty-seven different elementary schools. He dropped out after the eighth grade and never went to high school. During weekends while still in school, César worked the fields with his father and brothers. His father did not passively accept the exploitation of farm workers and joined fledgling agricultural unions that, regrettably, did not succeed. He also remembers discrimination in the schools against him and other Mexican American students as well as discrimination in public facilities. He especially noted not being allowed to sit in the main section of the only theater in Delano, California, in the Central Valley. César, influenced by his parents' teaching against prejudice, on one occasion refused to sit in the side aisles and instead sat in the center. He was arrested and released with a warning, but Cesar knew he had done no wrong. What was wrong was this type of public discrimination against people of Mexican descent.

After working with his parents in the fields for a few years, César enlisted in the Navy in 1944 when he turned seventeen. By now, of course, World War II was raging. He saw service in the Pacific but with little actual combat. Upon being released two years later, he returned to Delano in the Central Valley of California, where his family had more permanently settled. It was upon returning that he married his girlfriend Helen Fabela.

Soon thereafter César and Helen along with their developing family that would include eight children moved to urban San Jose, where they lived in an eastside barrio called "Sal Si Puedes" or "Get Out If You Can." César would later turn that around to invent his famous mantra "Sí Se Puede" ("Yes it can be done"). Working at different jobs including one at a lumber mill, César as a devout Catholic met Fr. Donald McDonnell at his local church. Fr. Donald, who had been working with Mexican Americans and with migrant workers, recognized certain leadership qualities in César and took him under his wing. He took on the responsibility of completing the education that César had never had. But it was a special kind of education centered in Fr. Donald's own personal interest in social justice and nonviolence. He gave César copies of key social justice doctrines of the Catholic Church such as *Rerum Novarum* (On the Condition of Labor). Issued in 1891 by Pope Leo XIII, this encyclical or papal pronouncement focused on the importance of providing dignity and respect to the new industrial labor force created by industrial capitalism in western Europe and the United States. This theme, of course, would become a major emphasis of César's future work with farm workers. In addition, Fr. Donald had César read the biography of Gandhi by Louis Fischer. César was highly impressed by Gandhi's use of nonviolence as not only a moral principle, but as a key strategy that successfully achieved the independence of India from the British Empire in the late 1940s. Nonviolence would, in turn, become a central tenet of the farm workers' struggle. As a Franciscan, Fr. Donald further impressed on César the life story of St. Francis, especially Francis's embracing of sacrificing for others. Influenced by St. Francis, César would likewise sacrifice his own life for the liberation of his people. The education of César Chávez by Fr. Donald would have a profound impact on the direction of this young Mexican American's life and on his evolving spirituality. It reinforced many of the same principles that his mother and grandmother had taught him: nonviolence, helping those in need, sacrificing for others, respect for others and for one's self.

It was Fr. Donald who also was responsible for César meeting another key influence on his life: Fred Ross. Ross was a community organizer for the Chicago-based Industrial Areas Foundation, which since the war had been active in organizing in labor and minority communities. In California, Ross helped organize the Community Service Organization (CSO) among Mexican Americans in the urban areas. The CSO spearheaded voter registration drives to increase the Mexican American vote and to elect candidates supportive of the Mexican American communities including Mexican American candidates. In its most successful campaign, the CSO helped to elect Edward Roybal in 1949 to the Los Angeles city council. Roybal became the first Mexican American to sit in this chamber since 1881. In addition to electoral politics, the CSO further promoted community organizing on issues such as police brutality, the improvement of public facilities such as streets and sidewalks in the barrios, and greater access to educational, housing, and medical facilities.

Fr. Donald impressed upon Ross that in César he might find an excellent potential new community organizer. César, at first, shied away from Ross, but eventually met him and was very impressed by Ross's organizing tactics as César accompanied the organizer to several house meetings in the barrio. César had found his mission in life. He would become a community organizer. Just as Fr. Donald had furthered the spiritual training that would be the seedbed of his work, Fred Ross taught César how to organize people around issues that mattered to them. But the two were interrelated. César's spirituality was based on his love of and care for others and their liberation from poverty and oppression. César would come to practice his version of the liberation theology that came out of Latin American Catholic circles in the 1960s in response to the reforms of Vatican Council II called by Pope John XXIII to make the Church more relevant to the modern world. Many in the Latin American Church believed that this relevance made it imperative for the Church to side with the all too many poor in the region and thus to proclaim a "preferential option for the poor." César was not schooled in liberation theology, but he practiced it nonetheless. The combination of Fr. Donald and Fred Ross is critical in appreciating the emergence of César as a major leader among Mexican Americans.

What Ross taught César was what came to be labeled the Alinsky method of organizing. It was Saul Alinsky in Chicago who had started the Industrial Areas Foundation (IAF). It was his organizing methods that were the key to the IAF's success. These methods included the following five principles. You had to organize around people's experiences. You had to communicate with the people. You had to bring out the contradictions of the system (you worked within the system but not with it). You had to take the moral high ground. Finally, you had to put pressure on the system. César learned this method in the 1950s and later applied it in his work with farm workers.

Besides learning the Alinsky method, César through Ross became a member of the CSO in 1953 and organized among Mexican Americans in different urban areas of California, including San Jose and Oxnard. His skills as an organizer and his commitment to social justice eventually elevated him to the head of the CSO in California.

But César never forgot his rural and farm worker's roots. He always carried the desire to help organize farm labor. However, others in the CSO believed that the organization was not sufficiently ready to venture into this area, where organizing would be much more difficult. César became discouraged and frustrated over the CSO's hesitancy and in 1962 left it and ventured into the fields once again. He knew it would be hard to organize a union of farm workers, and there would be major opposition by the growers. He would have few allies. Still, he had that dream and hope that it could be done. He knew in his soul that it could be done. Besides dealing with the various problems and forms of exploitation of farm workers, César also had to confront two other significant obstacles. One was that farm workers were not covered under the National Labor Relations Act, which in 1935 granted the right to industrial workers to unionize but at the behest of the agricultural industry had not extended such a right to farm workers. Second, since 1942 growers had access to the Bracero Program, which provided them with contract labor from Mexico. This had begun as a wartime measure but was extended thereafter. The availability of braceros made it more difficult to organize in the fields since braceros were only a temporary work force and could be used as strikebreakers.

Despite these obstacles, César, along with Helen, their families, and a small number of supporters, began organizing. This included the addition of Dolores Huerta, a dynamic and articulate Mexican American woman from Stockton who also had worked with the CSO. Dolores would go on to become a major leader in her own right in the UFW and the chief negotiator with the growers.

Together César and this small band of committed organizers launched in 1962 the National Farm Workers Association in the San Joaquin Valley with headquarters in Delano. They choose Delano not for any political reason, but because this was where both César and Helen had family, and César knew that they would need to fall back on family when they had no jobs or income to sustain them as they attempted to organize the workers.

Slowly but deliberately, César and the others in the evenings and on weekends began to meet with workers and their families in their homes to discuss the importance of a union and what it could do for them. As they began to recruit some members and to gather some dues, the union began to operate various services for the workers. Never a traditional union, what became the UFW offered various services such as a credit union, a cooperative food store, a gas station, and a drugstore, and provided burial insurance. In this sense the UFW was more similar to the older *mutualistas* or mutual benefit societies that Mexican immigrants had organized in the early twentieth century. To publicize its work, the union also published a newspaper, *El Malcriado* ("the unruly one or the upstart").

After almost three years of organizing, César and the union were confronted with a new challenge. A smaller union of predominantly Filipino workers affiliated with the AFL-CIO decided to go on strike against the major table grape growers in the Central Valley. They approached César and asked for his union to join the strike. César was initially not sure that his members were ready for what would be a major action. On the other hand, by 1965 the Bracero Program had finally been terminated, and this might be the opening that he was looking for to confront the growers. He decided to take the issue to his members.

Undoubtedly, César had already made up his own mind to join the strike because he scheduled the meeting for September 16, 1965, Mexican Independence Day. It would mark the day that farm workers could also declare their own independence from their subaltern status. The members agreed, voting overwhelmingly to join the Filipinos in striking. This would become the longest strike in U.S. agricultural history, lasting five long years. Yet one cannot understand this significant struggle by interpreting it only as a labor one. This was also a spiritual struggle enveloped by Mexican American Catholic beliefs, symbols, and traditions. It was not only a bread-and-butter campaign, but also one for the souls of the workers.

As the strike progressed and hundreds if not thousands of workers now affiliated with the union went on strike, César understood that part of the struggle would be to get media attention not only in California but nationally. He came up with the idea of a march from Delano to Sacramento in the spring of 1966. Here one sees the influence of the black civil rights marches. However, César didn't see this as just a political or labor march. He saw it as a *peregrinación* or pilgrimage. As a devout Catholic, César embraced the concept of a penitential pilgrimage to atone for one's sins and to strengthen one's faith. He knew that his predominantly Mexican American Catholic adherents also believed in this practice. This is how César considered the march to Sacramento. This would be not only a personal pilgrimage but a collective one. He knew that the strike would be long and hard. The *peregrinación* would prepare the farm workers for this.

With the banner of Our Lady of Guadalupe at the head of the pilgrimage accompanied by the U.S. and Mexican flags, César, the farm workers, and their supporters, especially from the Catholic, Protestant, and Jewish faiths, marched for twenty-five days to Sacramento. The image of Guadalupe had a special importance. She, as the mother of Jesus, who, according to the story, appeared as a perceived Indian virgin to the lowly Indian Juan Diego in 1531, represented a particular Mexican Catholic saint. Mexicans had always appealed to *la Virgen* for protection and, in time, for their independence from Spain in 1821. Almost one hundred years later, the revolutionaries also embraced her and carried her image into battle against the dictator Porfirio Díaz in the Mexican Revolution of 1910. In the 1960s, César and the farm workers would further appeal to her for support. As a way of also stressing the importance of faith in the farm workers' struggle, he planned the pilgrimage to conclude during Holy Week and to arrive in Sacramento on Easter Sunday. César and the workers had suffered, but the resurrection was at hand.

The pilgrimage, as César hoped, brought much media attention to the strike. Yet he knew that marches alone would not bring the growers to the bargaining table. Only pressure, especially economic pressure, would do this. César proposed a boycott of table grapes. Such a boycott is considered a secondary boycott prohibited by the antilabor revisions to the National Labor Relations Act passed by a conservative Republican Congress in the immediate post–World War II period. It was part of the effort to roll back the New Deal reforms. However, as a brilliant organizer, César knew that his farm workers' union could conduct a secondary boycott because farm labor was excluded from the law. He used the law against itself. Thus in early 1968 commenced the famous grape boycott that became a national and international boycott. César dispatched farm workers to organize the boycott in different cities and even in Canada and Europe. Many had never been out of California, but César assured them that they could do this. With the names of labor and religious people who might help them, the boycott representatives, paid only $5 a week, successfully plotted the boycott. Over the next two years, various city councils and other local governing bodies throughout the country and abroad voted to endorse the boycott. In addition, hundreds of college students and high school students, many of them Chicanos, picketed supermarkets in their communities to convince consumer not to buy nonunion grapes. The impact was significant. The sale of table grapes decreased dramatically.

Despite the success of the boycott, the union still underwent many hard times, and workers began to doubt that they could win. Some even began to consider more direct actions against the growers, possibly even violence. César got wind of these rumblings. Personally and politically committed to nonviolence, learned from his parents and from his attraction to both Gandhi and Dr. King, César decided that he had to do something to reemphasize the importance of nonviolence that he had early committed the movement to support. Further expressing the influence of Gandhi, he decided to go on a twenty-five-day fast in 1968 to suffer for the principle of nonviolence. He moved into a small shelter on the union's property of the Forty Acres and fasted and prayed. Masses and interfaith services were held for him. Soon hundreds of farm workers and supporters came to visit him and to join in partial fasting with him. César's fast squashed what dissent had appeared. A weak and exhausted but spiritually strengthened Chávez ended his fast on March 10, 1968, at an outdoor Mass. Using the occasion as both a religious and political occasion, César invited Senator Robert Kennedy to join him as he broke his fast by taking Holy Communion. Kennedy had been the first important national politician to endorse the strike. As they both received Communion, the symbolism could not have been more striking. Here was a poor farm labor organizer of Mexican American Catholic background alongside a wealthy Irish American Catholic politician, the heir to the Kennedy legacy. César knew that to defeat the growers the farm workers needed allies from other sectors. His joint Communion with Bobby Kennedy symbolized the achievement of this alliance. Senator Kennedy's assassination a few months later after his stunning victory in the California Democratic presidential primary deeply shocked César. He and the union had worked hard for Kennedy's victory and hoped to see him in the White House. The assassination was a temporary setback. César and the farm workers had lost a close and personal friend.

But César and the union carried on. By the summer of 1970 the boycott was hurting the growers in the pocketbook. They finally decided to negotiate. On July 29, 1970, in Delano, the union signed negotiated contracts with the leading grape growers in the San Joaquin Valley. Victory had been achieved. César's mantra of "Sí Se Puede" had been realized. It was a historical achievement. It marked the first time that farm workers in the United States had successfully unionized. One year earlier César had graced the cover of *Time* magazine, the first Mexican American ever to do so. It was a foretaste of victory. He was now a nationally recognized labor and civil rights leader. It was a collective victory, but there was no question of the indispensable role of César's leadership.

Yet the struggle continued. After the initial contracts expired, the growers refused to re-sign. In other locations in California, the union, renamed in 1972 the United Farm Workers (UFW), was challenged by the Teamsters Union, which competed to organize farm workers. Grow-ers were disposed to deal with the more conservative Teamsters. As a result, jurisdictional battles ensued between the UFW and the Team-sters, with some violence on the part of the Teamsters. In the end, both unions signed a pact allowing the Teamsters to organize packing shed workers while the UFW focused on field workers. Still, growers proved to be more recalcitrant to negotiate with César. Lettuce boycotts com-menced, followed by additional grape boycotts during the 1970s and 1980s. The UFW would win some contracts and lose some. Attempts by the 1980s and 1990s to stimulate the idealism of Americans to sup-port the struggle of farm workers seemed to no longer work as effec-tively. To bring attention to the struggle, César would go on numerous and extensive fasts that undoubtedly hurt his health. Yet *la lucha*—the struggle—continued.

***

There is no doubt that despite César Chávez's reputation as an Ameri-can Gandhi, his glory years encompassed the five-year struggle that cli-maxed in the first union contracts for farm workers. In this period, the genius as well as the moral commitment of César is clearly visible. To understand the success of the movement one needs to understand César's organizing themes and strategies, many of them influenced by his spirituality.

To begin with, César first and foremost stressed the dignity of farm workers and their right to unionize. In this effort, he did not believe in spontaneity; the achievement of providing a union that would promote the dignity of its members would not just happen or somehow be wished into existence. It had to be organized. César believed in organ-ization. He understood the need for leadership, but he attempted to fos-ter leadership from the bottom up, allowing the farm workers them-selves to assert their leadership. To this end, he worked to include whole families in the structure of the union so that everyone would feel a part of the movement.

Understanding the ethnic background of his mostly Mexican Amer-ican members and that of the general farm labor force in California, César utilized specific ethnic symbols to appeal to this population. For example, he used a revised symbol of the eagle on the Mexican flag for the UFW banner. According to César, when the eagle finally flew, it would mean that the farm workers were free of injustice. Moreover, the red and black colors of the banner are the exact colors of the labor movement in Mexico. He referenced Emiliano Zapata, the great leader of the campesino or peasant forces in the Mexican Revolution of 1910, and his mantra "*Tierra y Libertad*" (Land and Liberty). Spanish terms such as *huelga* (strike) and *La Causa* (the cause) became popular slogans among the strikers and their supporters. The union sponsored a theater group led by Luis Valdez called El Teatro Campesino (The Farm Workers' Theater) to dramatize the struggle. Of course, César employed the image of the Virgen de Guadalupe, not only the patroness of Mexico and of the Americas, but historically in Mexico the symbol of liberation movements. These ethnic symbols helped galvanize the workers and stressed that the union was their union and related to their Mexican ethnicity and historical and cultural traditions. As a by-product of César's use of ethnic symbols, this helped to foster the cultural nationalism that would characterize the Chicano movement. Ironically, he never saw himself as a cultural nationalist and indeed was wary of such movements. Instead, he saw himself in ecumenical terms appealing to a wide range of supporters. He understood, like any good political leader, that he had to first secure his base, but he also was astute enough to realize that Mexican American farm workers could not win their struggle on their own. They needed a coalition of supporters from various ethnic and religious backgrounds to do so. He felt the same way about the Chicano movement, although many in the movement did not heed his warning.

Besides ethnic symbols, César very profoundly utilized religious ones as a way of reaching out to the workers and to express the spiritual nature of the struggle. The Virgen de Guadalupe, as noted, played a prominent role in this respect. César had a special devotion to the Virgen and sought her protection in the farm workers' movement. In 1972 when he moved the union's headquarters from Delano to La Paz in the Tehachapi Mountains east of Bakersfield, he further expressed his Marian devotion by calling the new location La Paz after Our Lady of Peace. The employment of a *peregrinación* further stressed the role of religion in the cause. César labeled the 1966 pilgrimage to Sacramento as "Penitence, Pilgrimage, and Revolution." The anthem of the union was

"De Colores," a religious song that came out of the Cursillo movement of the 1950s and 1960s, which stressed the development of Catholic male lay leadership through spiritual retreats. César, himself, had been a cursillista. His fasting was always clothed in religious symbolism. In the marches and demonstrations, César invariably held public Masses for the people. Finally, he reached out and encouraged clergy, Catholic, Protestant, and Jewish, to join the movement. These expressions of religious sentiment and spirituality reflected not only César's own deep faith, but his political awareness that linking religion to the struggle was one effective way of blunting the charge that he and his movement were Communist inspired. This worked, for how could the Virgen de Guadalupe be a Communist?

To further appeal to a broad base of support, César in his organizing stressed that his union movement was not just a labor struggle, but also a movement for social justice. He knew that in the 1960s, most Americans would not be receptive to just a basic bread-and-butter labor effort. Most Americans by then saw labor unions as big, bureaucratic, corrupt, and part of the status quo. Moreover, César never saw his union in these traditional terms. He struggled not just for labor rights, but also for human rights, civil rights, and, above all, for the dignity of the workers. "Our union is not just another union," he proclaimed. "It is a movement . . . to change the conditions of human life."

Reflecting Gandhi and Dr. King and based on his own family socialization, César further organized his movement based on the principle of nonviolence. He believed that only a nonviolent movement would attract members to the union, and, as importantly, attract the wider public so needed especially to support the boycott. Yet nonviolence to César did not mean being passive and turning the other cheek. César instead proposed what he called "militant nonviolence." This meant that rather than a passive movement, the farm workers' struggle would be active and militant in putting pressure on the growers and their supporters in a nonviolent way such as the boycott. Of César's adherence to nonviolence, the critic Richard Rodriguez has written, "Chávez was a Gandhi without an India."

Other organizing tactics and strategies that Chávez brilliantly exploited included his keen awareness of the power of the mass media. He knew that in the age of television news that he needed to get his movement on television. His use of the concept of pilgrimage, with the marchers carrying the colorful banner of the union plus the image of Our Lady of Guadalupe, in addition to the faces of the farm workers themselves with so much character, attracted the lenses of the cameras. His public fasting and his public ending of his fasts, such as the orchestrated 1968 one with Senator Kennedy, again represented mass media spectacles. It was through the mass media plus the moral nature of his crusade that César reached and touched many Americans throughout the country who otherwise might never have given a second thought to farm workers. In addition, César was a pragmatist and not an ideologue. His organizing was built on what could reasonably be achieved. This reflected his CSO experience. Moreover, César understood the importance of leadership. Some later criticized him for being too "hands on" for all aspects of the union. Yet, certainly in the initial struggle, the moment called for the strong but committed leadership that César represented. He was the epitome of Gramsci's "organic intellectual." That is, despite his lack of formal education, César educated others, certainly the farm workers, by his actions.

All of these different organizing concepts and strategies came together in the first successful mass unionization drive among farm workers in U.S. history. This organization, in turn, reflected not only the astuteness of a major labor leader such as César, but his deep moral vision and his faith. None of these strategies would have succeeded without his faith in his God and in the dignity of his fellow human beings.

***

The literature on César Chávez and the farm workers' movement that he led is now rather voluminous. Both popular and scholarly studies stress primarily the labor, political, and civil rights aspects of the struggle. However, what has been sorely lacking is attention to César's spiritual nature, his Catholic persona, and how this influenced the UFW. César Chávez, I contend, was one of the great spiritual leaders in contemporary U.S. history. As he himself explained when asked how after many years of struggling he was able to continue, "Today I don't think that I could base my will to struggle on cold economics or on some political doctrine. I don't think there would be enough to sustain me. For me the base must be faith." It is this aspect of who César was that this book seeks to stress. It complements the recent excellent book by Fred-erick John Dalton, *The Moral Vision of César Chávez*, which is the first important study to focus on César's spirituality. Dalton's text is a schol-arly one that explores the various aspects of this spirituality or what he calls the moral vision of César. My focus is the same; however, the dif-ference is that my text is structured around César's own reflections on his spirituality. We read directly, unmediated by a scholar, the words of César about his faith.

And what was his faith all about? César's spiritually was structured around several key themes that represent the organization of my text. First and foremost was the spiritual training that he received as a child at the hands of his mother and grandmother. This religious socializa-tion in the Mexican American context has been referred to by some Latino theologians as *"abuelita* theology" or the theology of the grand-mothers. It is the popular theology, the people's theology apart from that of the official Catholic Church. In Mexican American and in other Latino cultures (and, of course, in other Catholic ethnic ones), it is the women of the family, the mothers and grandmothers (the *abueli-tas*), who are the gatekeepers of the faith. It is they who sustain the Catholic faith within the home by their devotions, by their prayers, by their home altars (*altarcitos*), by their personal commitment to certain saints and especially to Our Lady of Guadalupe, and, of course, by their socialization of the children to this faith. César acknowledged this. *Abuelita* theology thus is at the base of César's faith.

César's reflections on his spirituality further cover the following top-ics as organized in this text: the power of faith, human dignity, the poor, self-sacrifice, social justice, nonviolence, Gandhi, pilgrimage, fasting, prayer and meditation, love, humility, truth, the Virgen de Guadalupe, the spirituality of combating racism, the spirituality of nondiscrimina-tion, ecumenism and brotherhood, and death.

These different aspects of César Chávez's spirituality are very much a part of who he was. It is this part of César that this book seeks to re-veal. Some of his followers saw him as a saint. Some theologians refer to him as a mystic. Perhaps he was a saint and a mystic, but he was above all a man of deep faith, and it was this faith, this spirituality that guided him in his life and work. He needs to be remembered for this as well.

***

I want to share with you some of my own personal reflections on César Chávez. I did not know him personally very well. Of course, as he did for those of my generation—the Chicano Generation of the 1960s—he served as an inspiration. His leadership and struggle motivated the new generation of Mexican Americans, proudly and defiantly calling themselves the barrio term "Chicano." Many received their baptism in political activism by making their own personal *peregrinación* to Delano to meet César and to see how they could help *la causa*. Many then returned to their communities to support the grape boycott as well as to launch the urban-based Chicano movement. Drawing from César's courage, tactics, and use of ethnic symbols, this new generation of Chicano activists went on to organize their own urban-based movements. Combining civil rights issues with a militant assertion of their newly discovered identity as Chicanos, the Chicano Generation challenged the system on the meaning of democracy, a Chicano meaning based on an equitable sharing of the nation's wealth and privileges and respect and equality of opportunity for all ethnic groups. This challenge would be manifested in educational struggles, political representation, an anti-Vietnam War movement, struggles against police brutality and legal discrimination, protection for undocumented immigrants, equal rights for Chicana women, and a Chicano cultural and literary renaissance including the establishment of Chicano studies programs in universities.

I became "Chicano" in this period. As a graduate student at the University of California, San Diego, and as an instructor of history and Chicano studies at both San Jose State University and San Diego State University during the late 1960s and early 1970s, I participated in some aspects of Chicano movement politics. Part of this was supporting the farm workers. I would see and meet César during this time, as he would often speak on college campuses. Later, after I received my doctorate in history and accepted an appointment at the University of California, Santa Barbara, I would again see César over the years as he visited UCSB to speak to large audiences about the continued strikes and boycotts, and increasingly about the harmful effects of pesticides in the fields that harmed the workers and harmed consumers. An environmentalist, César was far ahead of his time. On some of these occasions, he would meet with smaller groups of Chicano students and faculty. These were occasions where I could shake his hand and welcome him as well as express support. At other times, César would also speak at La Casa de La Raza, the main Chicano community center in Santa Barbara. In fact, on one of these visits, César allowed me to take a picture of my young children, Giuliana and Carlo, together with him. I cherish that photo.

Later in the early 1990s when I briefly taught at Yale University, some of the Chicano students through their organization, MEChA, wanted to invite César to speak on campus. However, they had trouble raising the funds to pay for his travel. As director of ethnic studies, I assisted them with the funding that made it possible for them to bring César to campus. The students honored me by asking that I introduce him. This was a highlight for me. I welcomed him to a packed audience of students, faculty, and staff. He talked about the ongoing work of the union, the second grape boycott, and the dangers of pesticides. Afterward, I helped to escort him to one of the old and hallowed buildings at Yale, where you could smell tradition and where the portraits of past faculty and administrators watched guardedly over the facility. The scene was filled with contrasts. Here was César, a small, Indian-looking, modest leader of farm workers with his usual checkered shirt, the kind you buy at Penney's or Sears, in this elite and smug environment. The image remains vivid in my memory.

One has to remember that despite César's legendary status over the many years of his struggle he was not the usual image of a charismatic and vociferous leader. He was anything but that. He was a very modest and humble farm worker with little formal education who spoke softly and with little emotion. It was hard to look at him superficially and believe that he was one of the most important labor and civil rights leaders in the country's history. Yet he was. His personal power and influence were internal. It had to do, I believe, with his spirituality. He radiated a certain spiritual quality. You sensed that this was a man of principles. Indeed, we now realize that these were principles based on his deep faith.

The next time I encountered César regrettably was at his funeral. He died on April 23, 1993. His funeral was a week later in Delano. Thousands attended. Many were farm workers or the children and grandchildren of farm workers. Many were veterans of the UFW struggles and of the Chicano movement. High school and college students were bussed in by their schools. Political and religious figures attended, such as representatives of the Kennedy family, Jesse Jackson, former California governor Jerry Brown, and many others. Cardinal Roger Mahony of Los Angeles said the Mass. I went with a colleague and two graduate students. It was an eventful day. It was not somber. People were celebrating the life and contributions of César. The UFW flag with its bold eagle was quite visible, as were other signs and banners. It was as if the early days of the union were being reenacted. It was a hot and dusty day in the Central Valley that made the long funeral march that resembled the *peregrinación* of 1966 rather difficult. But as in any pilgrimage one expects to suffer, and so we did, remembering what César himself had suffered and what he had given to us. When it all concluded toward late afternoon, we were exhausted, thirsty, and hungry, but we knew—I knew—that we had to be there. This was history and collective memory, and I had to be a part of it. Through César's life we examined our own. His death reminded us about our own legacy and our own mortality. César's spirit and his spirituality were with us that day, and that is very much a part of his legacy. This is part of the motivation for this book.

***

Let me say a word about how I compiled César's reflections on his spirituality. As noted, the literature on César and the farm workers' movement is extensive. I focused on reviewing some of the more substantial studies as well as a number of journal and newspaper articles that contained interviews with César or statements and editorials by him. I read these looking for quotes that expressed his spirituality. I was not disappointed. In many of these publications, César is quoted concerning his views on the range of spiritual topics addressed in this book. I then collected these reflections and catalogued them under particular topics. I retained the original quotes except for some minor editorial adjustments. Some quotes, such as his reflections on nonviolence or self-sacrifice, are much more extensive than others. Still, together they provide a panorama of his spiritual views.

Moreover, from the outset I did not want to do a strictly academic book on César's spirituality. The Dalton book already is an excellent analysis of this topic. What I had in mind from the very beginning was to produce a book of spiritual reflections, almost of prayers or mantras, from one of the great secular spiritual leaders of our time. It is meant to inspire readers to reflect themselves on these different topics and on their own spirituality. You can start reading and contemplating almost anywhere in the book. Every quote is filled with serious reflection.

What I personally take away from this exercise is a deep appreciation of how much a moral and spiritual leader César Chávez was. He truly represents a popular theologian or what could be termed an "organic theologian." My goal is to further the integration of César Chávez into the canonical texts of U.S. history, something that still has not been completely accomplished. And in doing so, to impress upon others that you cannot fully understand César without understanding the spiritual core of his life and work. But at the same time, this is not a text aimed only at academics. It is intended for the general public of all backgrounds seeking spiritual guidance and hopefully finding it in César Chávez.

CHAPTER ONE

~

Abuelita or GrandmotherTheology

In Chicano/Latino religious culture, matriarchal figures, such as *abueli-
tas* or grandmothers and mothers, within the home are the mainstays of
preserving and passing on religious traditions and practices. They func-
tion as "live-in ministers." It is the women who socialize the children
about their faith, in most cases Catholicism. These influences are centered on popular religiosity that is the religion that the people practice
apart in many cases from the institutionalized Church. These practices
have their origins in Mexico or Central America, especially in the rural areas where often there is a scarcity of priests, and so the people
themselves observe their religion within their homes and in the community without the aid of clergy. These forms of popular religion often
associated with what Latino theologians in the United States refer to
as *abuelita theology* include the use of *altarcitos* or home altars, where
daily prayers are recited and which contain a variety of religious icons
such as pictures of Our Lady of Guadalupe, the patron saint of Mexico
and among Mexican Americans, as well as photos of family members
who are away especially in the military. *Abuelita* theology also involves
saying the rosary at home, teaching the Bible, parental blessings, and a
variety of other religious forms of education offered by grandmothers
and mothers to their children. The following quotes by César Chávez

25

indicate that he and his siblings received their initial religious influences within the home from their mother and grandmother. It is
abuelita theology that is at the core of César's spirituality.

***

"[My] mother would tell us, 'You always have to help the needy, and
God will help you.'"[1]

"My mother had a reputation in the valley for her skill in healing, a
skill she put to constant use, for she couldn't bear to see anyone in
pain, and there were no doctors in the [North Gila] valley. She was especially knowledgeable in the use of herbs, choosing some to cool a
fever, others to cure colic, and mixing brews for specific illnesses. Her
faith in her skill was as strong as her belief in the saints and the Virgin of Guadalupe."[2]

"As we didn't have a Church in the valley and it was very difficult to go
to Yuma, it was my mother who taught us prayers. Throughout the
Southwest and Mexico where there were no priests for a long time, the
amazing thing was that people kept the faith. She believed in saints as
advocates, as lobbyists, to pray to God for her. Her patron saint was St.
Eduvigis, a Polish duchess who, in the early Christian era, gave up all of
her worldly possessions, distributed them among the poor, and became
a Christian. On the saint's birthday, October 16, my mom would find
some needy person to help and, until recently, she would always invite
people to the house, usually hobos. She would go purposely to look for
someone in need, give him something, and never take anything in return. Usually they would offer to do some work, like chop wood in ex-
change for a meal, but she would refuse because, she said, the gift then
was invalid. I think that is a very beautiful custom, and my dad must
have felt pretty much the same way because he didn't object."[3]

"Mama Tella [grandmother] gave us our formal religious training. . . .
[S]he was always praying, just praying. Every evening she would sit in
bed, and we would gather in front of her. As we knelt by the doorway
to her room, we would join her in the Rosary that seemed to drone on

endlessly. We were required to kneel until the prayer was over, and if we started giggling, she would hit us with her cane. After the Rosary she would tell us about a particular saint and drill us on our Cate-chism."[4]

[Recalling his mother's attitude toward the poor:]
"[She] had made a pledge never to turn away anyone who came for food, and there were a lot of ordinary people who would come and a lot of hobos, at any time of the day or night. Most of them were white."[5]

[When family migrated up and down California in the 1940s:]
"On the road, no matter how badly off we were, she [mother] would never let us pass a guy or a family in trouble. Never. During the Second World War, we began to travel in groups. We'd pick up families that were new, that had just been dumped into the migrant stream. After we sort of had given them an apprenticeship, they felt confident, and they'd take off. My mother did a lot of this work. I didn't realize how important it was until years later. I didn't even understand what she was doing. In fact, I didn't particularly like the idea very much. The things she did, being unlettered, were really amazing, just dealing with the problems and trying to help people. And my dad gave her the backing that she needed. We didn't get anybody to help us like that in the be-ginning. That's why we suffered so much, but my mother would tell us, 'You always have to help the needy, and God will help you.'"[6]

"She [mother] also gave us a lot of *consejos*—advice. . . . I remember her story of the stone freezing in the boy's hand. It was a very disobedient son who came home drunk and got real mad at his mother. He picked up a rock and was about to throw it at her when it froze to his hand. Her stories were about obedience and honesty and some of the virtues. There were others that dealt with miracles. The range was very wide."[7]

"Although my mother opposed violence, I think the thing that she re-ally cracked down on the most was being selfish. She made us share everything we had. If we had an apple or a tiny piece of candy, we had to cut it into five pieces."[8]

"My mom kept the family together. She was the sort of woman who had time for her children, who would talk with us. She used many *dichos*—proverbs—and they all had a real purpose. 'What you do to others, others do to you' was one of them. 'He who holds the cow, sins as much as he who kills her.' 'If you're in the honey, some of it will stick to you.' Though she was illiterate, she had a tremendous memory. I think most illiterate persons do because they must rely on their memories."[9]

[César recalled when his family first arrived in California and a kind lady helped them:]

"It was about Christmastime in Oxnard when my mother met Natividad Rodríguez. She was also from Arizona. People in the neighborhood said she was a loudmouth, but after we met her we found out her heart was in the right place. She had some shacks that she rented, one right up against another, just like a Casbah. It was raining dogs and cats one day when she saw us out in the tent.

"'What in the hell are you doing out here?' she asked my mother. When she was told we didn't have any money to rent, she said, 'Well, you better start packing up right now because you are going to move in with me!' Just like that.

"'We don't have any money,' my mother protested. 'I really would like to move in, but we don't have any money. My husband isn't working.'

"'Who in the hell is talking about money,' she said. 'Come with me. Let's go. Let's go see the house and see if you like it.'

"It was just a shack, just a roof, but there was a little heater inside, and it even had a wooden floor. We were excited. So my mother said it was fine, just beautiful.

"'Okay, you move in right now. Just don't mention rent. Just forget it. If you have any money, you can pay me. If you don't have money, you don't have to pay me.'

"So we stayed there with a roof over our heads for the rest of the winter."[10]

"When I look back, I see her [mother's] sermons had tremendous impact on me. I didn't know it was nonviolence then, but after reading Gandhi, St. Francis, and other exponents of nonviolence, I began to clarify that in my mind. Now that I'm older I see she is nonviolent, if anybody is, both by word and deed. She would always talk about not fighting. Despite a culture where you're not a man if you don't fight back, she would say, 'No, it's best to turn the other cheek. God gave you the senses like eyes and mind and tongue and you can get out of anything.' She would say, 'It takes two to fight.' That was her favorite. 'It takes two to fight, and one can't do it alone.' She had all kinds of proverbs for that. 'It's better to say that he ran from here than to say he died here.' When I was young I didn't realize the wisdom in her words, but it has been proved to me so many times since. Today I appreciate the advice, and I use quite a few of the *dichos*, especially in Spanish."[11]

"Sometimes the [labor] contractor would cheat the workers by putting his knee under the sack so it would weigh less. Instead of getting credited for a hundred-pound sack, the worker would get marked down for only eighty pounds. All this would happen pretty fast and the victim's view was usually blocked. Well, Mama was pretty sharp. She saw the contractor cheating a worker who was in line ahead of her, and she called him on it. The contractor was furious. The entire Chávez family got fired."[12]

"Since those days [childhood and youth], my need for religion has deepened."[13]

Notes

1. Jacques Levy, *Cesar Chavez: Autobiography of La Causa* (New York: W. W. Norton & Company, Inc., 1975), p. 70.

2. Levy, *Cesar Chavez*, p. 11.

3. Levy, *Cesar Chavez*, pp. 25–26.

4. Levy, *Cesar Chavez*, p. 26.

5. Richard Griswold del Castillo and Richard A. García, *César Chávez: A Triumph of Spirit* (Norman: University of Oklahoma Press, 1995), p. 5.

6. Levy, *Cesar Chavez*, p. 70.

7. Levy, *Cesar Chavez*, p. 18.

8. Levy, *Cesar Chavez*, p. 19.

9. Levy, *Cesar Chavez*, p. 18.

10. Levy, *Cesar Chavez*, p. 59.

11. Levy, *Cesar Chavez*, pp. 18–19.

12. Susan Ferriss and Ricardo Sandoval, *The Fight in the Fields: Cesar Chavez and the Farmworkers Movement* (New York: Harcourt Brace & Company, 1997), p. 251.

13. Frederick John Dalton, *The Moral Vision of César Chávez* (Maryknoll, NY: Orbis Books, 2003), p. 34.

CHAPTER TWO

~

Power of Faith

Learning his faith at home as well as in the Church, César Chávez came to possess a deep Catholic faith. It was not a static faith but one that evolved as he himself evolved. It was a faith based on his personal reverence for God and his embrace of the human dignity of all people, even his opponents. It was a faith that looked not just to a heavenly resurrection, but one that also focused on an earthly one through the struggle for social justice. As the first powerful quote in this section stresses, it was César's faith more than anything else that provided the strength for his long and arduous struggles. His movement of farm workers was first and foremost a faith-based movement because César understood the power of faith.

***

"Today I don't think that I could base my will to struggle on cold economics or on some political doctrine. I don't think there would be enough to sustain me. For me the base must be faith."[1]

"The only justice is Christ—God's justice. We're the victims of a lot of shenanigans by the courts but ultimately, down the line, real justice comes. It does not come from the courts, but it comes from a set of circumstances and I think God's hand is in it. God tends to write very straight with crooked lines."[2]

"To me, religion is a most beautiful thing. And over the years, I have come to realize that all religions are beautiful. Your religion just happens to depend a lot on your upbringing and your culture."[3]

"It's not necessary to have a religion to act selflessly. I know many agnostics who are more religious in their own way than most people who claim to be believers. While most people drawn toward liberation or radicalism leave the church, I went the other way. I drew closer to the Church the more I learned and understood."[4]

"[E]ven in the face of the biggest disappointment there's always that faith, that tomorrow's gonna be different."[5]

"It may be too simple to say Jesus is on our side; but we tend to feel that way perhaps [because] his identification with the oppressed is so clear to us because we do not have to rationalize our wealth and possessions and fit Jesus' deeds and words into the world view of the powerful and the affluent."[6]

"I think there are three elements to my faith. It's God, myself and my brother. I'm traditional. I'm Catholic traditional. I go to Church regularly and faithfully. . . . But besides that, I also have what I consider is a renewal religion. I go out and do things. That's what I think is a real faith, and that's what I think Christ really taught us: to go do something. We can look at His sermon [Sermon on the Mount] and it's very plain what He wants us to do: clothe the naked, feed the hungry and give water to the thirsty. It's very simple stuff and that's what we've got to do. In the union we have what we call our 'Social commitments' and those are things we do for other people not in the union. We commit ourselves to go help people outside, and everybody in the leadership has this commitment. For instance, today one of the leaders went over to the state prisoners. That's a commitment. Another one is going to the hospital. We've got to give our faith an essence through deeds."[7]

"Religion is a deep part of us. . . . Our religion and our life are insepa-
rable."[8]

"Sometimes people come and stay with us and complain, 'What, another Mass!' But after they are around us for a while and have a feeling
for our life they begin to ask 'How come you don't have a Mass today?'
. . . We try to live as a community. We have a feeling for St. Paul and
what he writes about the communities he struggled to build. The problem is that some outsiders cannot understand the rewards of this way of
life; they think we want to get out of it or change it radically. And that
is not true. We have a way of life and we want to live it without exploitation."[9]

"The strikers took a sacred oath to support the struggle. They solemnly
swore: 'I promise my honor in order to sustain the cause. God is my witness.'"[10]

Notes

1. Jacques Levy, *Cesar Chavez: Autobiography of La Causa* (New York: W.
W. Norton & Company, 1975), p. 27.
2. Frederick John Dalton, *The Moral Vision of César Chávez* (Maryknoll,
NY: Orbis Books, 2003), p. 80.
3. Levy, *Cesar Chavez*, p. 27.
4. Levy, *Cesar Chavez*, p. 27.
5. John C. Hammerback and Richard J. Jensen, *The Rhetorical Career of
César Chávez* (College Station: Texas A & M University Press, 1998), p. 30.
6. *National Catholic Reporter*, March 7, 1975.
7. *National Catholic Reporter*, March 14, 1982.
8. Hammerback and Jensen, *Rhetorical Career*, p. 30.
9. Dalton, *Moral Vision*, p. 45.
10. Dalton, *Moral Vision*, p. 98.

César Chávez, circa 1960s. UCLA Department of Special Collections, Charles E. Young Research Library.

CHAPTER THREE

~

Human Dignity

As part of his deep Catholic faith, César Chávez believed in the incarnational principle. That is, that God in becoming man through Jesus sanctified being human. Human beings share in the divine. As a result, in his struggle with the farm workers, César made it very clear that this struggle was not just for "bread and butter" and material gains. It was not just another labor movement. It was above all a struggle to achieve the God-given human dignity of farm workers. These were the lowliest of all workers in the United States. No one paid attention to them. Growers treated them as less than human. Paid less than living wages, enduring hard and long workdays, and living in run-down labor camps with few facilities and lack of availability of education for their children, farm workers were truly forgotten people. But because of his faith, César saw them differently. They were children of God made in His image. This is what César wanted to bring attention to. He struggled to improve the material lives of farm workers, but he also struggled for their human rights and for others to accept them as fellow human beings. Yet the workers themselves would also achieve human dignity, as some of these quotes in this section emphasize. Through their organizing in the union and through their picketing and marching, they would come to recognize their own humanity in each other.

***

"It really doesn't matter in the final analysis how powerful we are, how many boycotts we win, how many growers we sign up, or how much political clout we possess, if in the process we forget whom we are serving. We must never forget that the human element is the most important thing we have—if we get away from this, we are certain to fail."[1]

"There is nothing more shameful and perhaps more disgraceful than the man who offers to work for lower wages. . . . To cheapen oneself is a crime against human decency. . . . Work is a sacred thing, as are wages. Every individual is endowed with dignity. The work that this individual does merits just wages."[2]

"Our union is not just another union; [it is] a movement more than a union [that seeks] to change the conditions of human life. [For that reason] we resist giving our members numbers. Once we do that we are frightened that we will become one mass. Our people are human! They are not numbers!"[3]

"You must understand—I must make you understand—that our membership and the hopes and aspirations of the hundreds of thousands of the poor and dispossessed that have been raised on our account are, above all, human beings, no better and no worse than any other cross section of human society; we are not saints because we are poor, but by the same measures neither are we immoral. We are men and women who have suffered and endured much, and not only because of our abject poverty but because we have been kept poor. The color of our skin, the language of our cultural and native origins, the lack of formal education, the exclusion from the democratic process, the numbers of our slain in recent wars—all these burdens—generation after generation have sought to demoralize us, to break our human spirit. But God knows that we are not beasts of burden, agricultural implements or rented slaves; we are men locked in a death struggle against man's inhumanity to man. . . . And this struggle itself gives meaning to our life and ennobles our dying."[4]

"All men are brothers, sons of the same God; that is why we say to all men of good will, in the words of Pope Leo XIII: 'Everyone's first duty is to protect the workers from the greed of speculators who use human beings as instruments to provide themselves with money. It is neither just nor human to oppress with excessive work to the point where their minds become enfeebled and their bodies worn out.' God shall not abandon us!"[5]

"Many things in farm labor are terrible, like going under the vines that are sprayed with sulphur and other pesticides. You have to touch those leaves and inhale that poison. Then there are the heat and the short-handle hoes and the stooping over. So many jobs require stooping. They should find a way of doing this work that will leave the human being whole. I think it can be done, but it won't be until one or two things happen. Either the employers begin to see the workers as human beings, or the workers organize against the employers and demand changes."[6]

"In organizing people, you have to get across to them their human worth and the power they have in numbers."[7]

"In order to help the farm workers, look at them as human beings and not as something extra special, or else you are kidding yourselves and are going to be mighty, mighty disappointed. Don't pity them, either. Treat them as human beings, because they have just as many faults as you have; that way you'll never be in trouble, because you'll never be disappointed."[8]

"People come along that have a great deal of love of human beings and have never found a way to channel it. And then they go out on strike and transform that love into something effective—the whole question of human rights. Women have something very special this way; women have a lot of staying power. They're endowed with some real special thing by God, I think. Men, you know, we want it, let's do it, we want to finish it all up in seconds, but women just keep going. If you're full of *machismo*, you can't appreciate what women do, but if you're not, it's really beautiful."[9]

"They [farm workers] are important because of the work they do. They are not implements to be used and discarded. They are human beings who sweat and sacrifice to bring food to the tables of millions and millions of people throughout the world. They are important because God made them, gave them life, and cares for them in life and in death."[10]

"Human beings are unique because they are creative. When we stifle that creativity, we destroy the individual's spirit. We need to give workers a voice. Let them be creative at their place of work. Not only will that enrich their lives, but it will benefit us. We need work that improves the quality of life, for this type of work is the cornerstone of human dignity. And because people are important, working for people—even sacrificing a little bit for them—brings much meaning to one's life."[11]

"Our conviction is that human life is a very special possession given by God to men and that no one has the right to take it for any reason or for any cause, however just it may be."[12]

[When Chavez's family came to California and was exploited by labor contractors:]
    "And it's not so much the money, it's the whole principle of being cheated out of something you had to sweat so hard to earn. It is not like somebody stealing fifteen cents from you, it's like somebody stealing fifteen cents worth of hard labor, which is an entirely different thing. It's a matter of destroying your manhood, taking away all your dignity."[13]

"All my life, I have been driven by one dream, one goal, and one vision: To overthrow a farm labor system in this nation which treats farm workers as if they were not important human beings. That dream was born in my youth. It was nurtured in my early days of organizing. It has flourished."[14]

"[Farm workers] want to have our own federation, to be able to say 'yes' to our own dignity. Saying 'yes' to the farm worker's struggle is really saying 'yes' to . . . man's dignity because it is putting an ideal into action. . . . [W]e are saying 'yes' to life because that is what life is all about."[15]

"There are [a] few basic principles that I try to follow: Don't lie! And work hard! You can compromise in many things but not in your principles. You have to stay true to yourself. There are special guides that God gives you and you cannot trade them off. That's a sin; then you reap what you sow. You have to use these gifts in life or you miss everything."[16]

"We know that when human beings are concerned for one another, that the thing that all of us want when we're concerned for one another is to build and not to destroy. And we're concerned really for the dignity of man. We're saying that we're concerned not only for the guy that makes the headlines or the guy that has the money or the guy that has the good word. But we're concerned for the least of our own brothers. And we're concerned for human dignity. We're concerned for everyone and particularly concerned for the poor. And it's at this point then that I think that we realize that [we have] to struggle and to struggle very hard and to want to change things so we can get justice and dignity for our people."[17]

"When you go to people and you ask them to give you something, you have to go with your hands clean."[18]

"We raise two things here in Delano [1969]: grapes and slaves. But we will win with two weapons: dedication and disciplined sacrifice. And both of these are encased in the perfect case: the human being."[19]

"We made a solemn promise: to enjoy our rightful part of the riches of this land, to throw off the yoke of being considered as agricultural implements or slaves. We are free men and we demand justice."[20]

"One of the most beautiful and satisfying results of our work in establishing a union in the fields is in witnessing the worker's bloom—the natural dignity coming out of a man when his dignity is recognized. Workers . . . are blooming as capable, intelligent persons using initiative and showing leadership."[21]

"We must never forget that the human element is the most important thing we have—if we get away from this, we are certain to fail."[22]

"We need work that improves the quality of life, for this type of work is the cornerstone of human dignity. And because people are important, working for people—even sacrificing a little bit for them—brings much meaning to one's life."[23]

"To affiliate with a group is only the first step; to become an active member requires time and dedication. The organized farm worker develops the sense of human dignity, liberty, and the necessity of improving his standard of living. . . . In the brotherhood of the movement farm workers can obtain the dignity and respect they deserve. They can exercise the right that God has given them to obtain a better life for themselves and their families. To join a movement like this is one thing, but to become a true member is another. It requires understanding the purpose and goals of the labor movement. Furthermore, it requires faith in the dignity of man."[24]

"Rebel against the injustice of your grower. Revolt against the injustice of your labor contractor. God is witness that what you ask for is just. God is witness to the abuses that have been committed against you. God is witness and judge and will judge in the near future. All the abuses are against the dignity of man, who is made by God in his own image."[25]

"When a man or woman, young or old, takes a place on the picket line for even a day or two, he will never be the same again. He has confirmed his own humanity. Through nonviolence, he has confirmed the humanity of others."[26]

"It's always me and you and all people and God, never just me and God."[27]

[On anti-farm worker legislation:]
　　"My concern is the spirit of fear that lies behind such laws in the hearts of growers and legislators across the country. Somehow these powerful men and women must be helped to realize that there is nothing to fear from treating their workers as fellow human beings."[28]

"[The UFW is] fighting for our dignity, challenging and overcoming in-justice, and empowering the least educated and poorest among us."[29]

"We Mexicans here in the United States, as well as all other farm la-borers, are engaged in another struggle for the freedom and dignity which poverty denies us. But it must not be a violent struggle, even if violence is used against us."[30]

Notes

1. César Chávez, "Introduction," in Mark Day, *Forty Acres: Cesar Chavez and the Farm Workers* (New York: Praeger Publishers, 1971), p. 2.

2. Frederick John Dalton, *The Moral Vision of César Chávez* (Maryknoll, NY: Orbis Books, 2003), p. 97.

3. As quoted in "El Malcriado: The Voices of the Farm Worker," in Luis Valdez and Stan Steiner, eds., *Aztlan: An Anthology of Mexican American Liter-ature* (New York: Alfred A. Knopf, 1972), p. 208.

4. César Chávez, "Letter from Delano" [to E. L. Ban, president of Califor-nia Grape and Tree Fruit League in San Francisco], Good Friday, 1969, in Ed-mund Simmon, ed., *Pain and Promise: The Chicano Today* (New York: New American Library, 1972), p. 30.

5. "Plan de Delano," in Gilberto López y Rivas, ed., *The Chicano: Life and Struggles of the Mexican Minority in the United States* (New York: Monthly Re-view Press, 1973), p. 109.

6. Jacques Levy, *Cesar Chavez: Autobiography of La Causa* (New York: W. W. Norton & Company, 1975), p. 75.

7. "March of the Migrants," *Life*, April 29, 1966, pp. 93–94.

8. Peter Matthiessen, *Sal Si Puedes: Cesar Chavez and the New American Revolution* (New York: Random House, 1969), p. 115.

9. Matthiessen, *Sal Si Puedes*, p. 160.

10. César Chávez, "Inhuman Treatment of Farm Workers Must End," *Los Angeles Times*, February 11, 1974, p. 7.

11. Richard J. Jensen and John C. Hammerback, eds., *The Words of César Chávez* (College Station: Texas A & M University Press, 2002), p. 92.

12. Jensen and Hammerback, *Words of César Chávez*, p. 96.

13. Levy, *Cesar Chavez*, p. 61.

14. Jensen and Hammerback, *Words of César Chávez*, pp. 122–123.

15. Dalton, *Moral Vision*, p. 79.

16. Dalton, *Moral Vision*, p. 146.

17. Jensen and Hammerback, *Words of César Chávez*, p. 58.

18. Pat Hoffman, *Ministry of the Dispossessed: Learning from the Farm Worker Movement* (Los Angeles: Wallace Press, 1987), p. 71.

19. Winthrop Yinger, *César Chávez: The Rhetoric of Nonviolence* (Hicksville, NY: Exposition Press, 1975), p. 73.

20. Yinger, *César Chávez*, p. 63.

21. Yinger, *César Chávez*, p. 29.

22. Day, *Forty Acres*, p. 12.

23. Jensen and Hammerback, *Words of César Chávez*, p. 92.

24. Dalton, *Moral Vision*, p. 97.

25. Dalton, *Moral Vision*, p. 98.

26. Dalton, *Moral Vision*, pp. 127–128.

27. Dalton, *Moral Vision*, pp. 127–128.

28. Dalton, *Moral Vision*, p. 134.

29. Dalton, *Moral Vision*, pp. 164–165.

30. Richard Griswold del Castillo and Richard A. García, *César Chávez: A Triumph of Spirit* (Norman: University of Oklahoma Press, 1995), p. 44.

CHAPTER FOUR

~

On the Poor

As part of his struggle to bring human dignity to farm workers, César Chávez also stressed the self-worth and strength of poor people. He decried the poverty of farm workers but rejected the concept of the "culture of poverty" that suggested the hopelessness and self-defeating nature of the poor. For César, such concepts represented justifications for the perpetuation of poverty and the disempowerment of the poor. He countered these views and stereotypes by asserting the inner strength of the poor and their self-determination to overcome their conditions. He did not romanticize poverty—indeed he condemned it—but he championed the cause of the poor because they were God's special children. While he did not specifically refer to the concept of liberation theology sweeping Latin American in the 1960s and 1970s that called for a "preferential option for the poor" among Catholics, César in his own way represented a liberationist. His cause—like that of Jesus—was that of the poor and the marginalized. He dedicated his life to them and he was one of them.

***

"For us there is nowhere else to go. Although we would like to see victory come soon, we are willing to wait. In this sense time is our ally. We learned many years ago that the rich may have money, but the poor have time."[1]

"Time accomplishes for the poor what money does for the rich."[2]

"In the beginning, the UFW attacked the source of shame with which our people lived. We attacked injustice and poor living conditions, not by complaining, not by seeking hand-outs, not by becoming soldiers in the War on Poverty, but by organizing."[3]

[On forgiveness and change concerning a labor contractor who had exploited César's parents and others in Oxnard after the family arrived in California in the late 1930s:]
"In 1958 when I was back in Oxnard with the CSO, I ran into Fidel's father again. [Fidel had attended Our Lady of Guadalupe School with César and his brother, Richard, and was the son of the labor contractor.] At first I didn't know who he was. He was very old, broke, and just miserable. This lady, who was much younger than he was, came to see me for help. She turned out to be his wife. They were losing their house and were in bad shape. We had to prove he was eligible for aid, so I went to his home to get his whole history. His name didn't ring a bell until I went over the record and saw that he was a labor contractor. Then it hit me. I realized who he was, and I thought, should I help him? Those earlier days came back vividly, and I thought again, should I help him? My first impulse was to drop it, thinking of all the things he had done to us. But then I saw him in the other room sitting in a chair, wrapped in a blanket and very thin. As I looked at him, I saw how helpless he was. I didn't tell them I knew about him, I just said I knew how to help them. Eventually we settled the case, got him money for disability, got them some welfare payments, and got the real estate guy to wait for his payments—they were two payments behind. So we helped them. Soon after that he died."[4]

[During the early days when César was first organizing the National Farm Workers Association:]
"And the members we recruited were wonderful. During the season they would come thirty, forty miles and bring us beets, or celery, or car-

rots or chickens. They knew our condition, not because we told them, but because we were so intimately a part of them. They knew. They'd see the need and come running. The poor are great."[5]

"It is more than a union as we know it today that we have to build. It is a movement. It is a movement of the poor."[6]

"Every time I see lettuce, that's the first thing I think of, some human had to thin it. And it's just like being nailed to a cross. You have to walk twisted, or you're stooped over, facing the row, and walking perpendicular to it. You are always trying to find the best position because you can't walk completely sideways, it's too difficult, and if you turn the other way, you can't thin."[7]

"People are not going to turn back now. The poor are on the march: black, brown, red, everyone, white included. We are now in the midst of the biggest revolution this country has ever known. We shall strike; we shall organize boycotts; we shall demonstrate, and we shall have political campaigns. We shall pursue the revolution we have proposed. We are sons and daughters of the farm workers' revolution, a revolution of the poor seeking bread and justice."[8]

"We know that our cause is just, that history is a story of social revolution, and that the poor should inherit the land."[9]

"People who are hungry have no spirit, have no strength to fight. People who are hungry don't care who makes decisions for them, so long as their families don't starve. . . . People who are hungry have to eat first."[10]

"We are poor. Our allies are few. But we have something the rich do not own. We have our own bodies and spirits and the justice of our cause as our weapons."[11]

"On Thursday, November 28, all Americans except the poor will thank God for the abundance of good things this earth has produced. Little will know that the poor will be celebrating a different kind of Thanksgiving, a Thanksgiving of hope for the future when they, too, will enjoy similar blessings. It is ironic that those who till the soil, cultivate and harvest the fruits, vegetables and other foods that fill your tables with abundance have significantly less for themselves. This is very poignant at Thanksgiving."[12]

"The place to begin is with our own experience with the Church in the strike which has gone on for thirty-one months in Delano. For in Delano the Church has been involved with the poor in a unique way which should stand as a symbol to other communities. Of course, when we refer to the Church we should define the word a little. We mean the whole Church, the Church as an ecumenical body spread around the world, and not just its particular form in a parish in a local community. The Church we are talking about is a tremendously powerful institution in our society, and in the world. That Church is one form of the Presence of God on earth, and so naturally it is powerful. It is powerful by definition. It is a powerful moral and spiritual force which cannot be ignored by any movement. Furthermore, it is an organization with tremendous wealth. Since the Church is to be a servant to the poor, it is *our* fault if that wealth is not channeled to help the poor in our world."[13]

"When the poor speak of a well-educated man they don't mean schooling. A well-educated man to them is one who is sensitive and courteous to others."[14]

"Man has a great need to be of service but I think it is very hard for him when he gets too far away from mother earth. The farm worker has a tremendous sense of participation in nature's cycle. It is very satisfying, much more satisfying than better paying jobs on an assembly line where men are unhappy in their work. I think that is why so many revolutions are begun and won by rural people. They are the poorest and yet the most secure."[15]

[Regarding St. Francis of Assisi:]
    "He was one of the saints that I admired most because of his commitment. He looked at poverty as a godsend, not as a curse. He took

poverty and made it work for him so he could help other people. Also, what attracts me is his whole commitment to peace; not only peace where there's war but peace with oneself and one's Creator, peace with your surroundings and the environment."[16]

"Well, he [St. Francis] was involved with people and we're involved with people. . . . He had a faith that was overpowering, and he was willing to sacrifice himself to do good for people. That appeals to me. He comes into the union through those of us who think and really accept poverty. We've accepted poverty. We don't get wages, we don't have a home, a car. Most of the things we wear have been donated to us. We're not starving of course, but we're accepting at least that much, and so that's how he comes into us."[17]

"We found out many useful things after we began to not be so concerned with ourselves, and how we looked, what we ate, and what we said. And we began to find out a lot of beautiful things, how people really are, how the poorer they are, the more open they are, and the more beautiful they are. We also found out that while it's not beautiful to be poor if you have no choice, or just for the sake of being poor, it's beautiful to give up material things that take up your time, for the sake of time to help your fellow-human beings. I think that has a lot of beauty in it."[18]

"People must come to see assistance to one another as the purpose of the organization [UFW], as its very reason for being."[19]

"Our goal is a national union of the poor dedicated to world peace and serving the needs of all men who suffer."[20]

"Actually, I can't see where the poor have fared that well under any political or economic system. But I think some power has to come to them so they can manage their lives. I don't care what system it is, it's not going to work if they don't have the power."[21]

"In the beginning there was a lot of nonsense about the poor farm worker: 'Gee, the farm worker is poor and disadvantaged and on strike, he must be a super human being!' And I said, 'Cut that nonsense out.'

That was my opening speech: 'Look, you're here working with a group of men; the farm worker is only a human being. You take the poorest of these guys and give him that ranch over there, he could be just as much of a bastard as the guy sitting there right now. Or if you think that all growers are bastards, you're not good to us either. Remember that both are *men*. In order to help the farm workers, look at them as human beings and not as something extra special, or else you are kidding yourself and are going to be mighty, mighty disappointed. Don't pity them either. Treat them as human beings, because they have just as many faults as you have.'"[22]

"The time-worn struggle of the poorest of the poor, the farm worker, the men and women who work from sunrise till sunset in the cold winter, and under the searing heat of the sun in summer . . . so that they, too, will enjoy the kind of life that Americans already enjoy; their struggle has brought us very close to each other."[23]

Notes

1. Richard J. Jensen and John C. Hammerback, eds., *The Words of César Chávez* (College Station: Texas A & M University Press, 2002), p. 97.

2. Mark Day, *Forty Acres: Cesar Chavez and the Farm Workers* (New York: Praeger Publishers, 1971), p. 77.

3. Frederick John Dalton, *The Moral Vision of César Chávez* (Maryknoll, NY: Orbis Books, 2003), p. 80.

4. Jacques Levy, *Cesar Chavez: Autobiography of La Causa* (New York: W. W. Norton & Company, 1975), pp. 57–58.

5. Levy, *Cesar Chavez*, p. 170.

6. John C. Hammerback and Richard J. Jensen, *The Rhetorical Career of César Chávez* (College Station: Texas A & M University Press, 1998), pp. 82–83.

7. Levy, *Cesar Chavez*, p. 74.

8. Jensen and Hammerback, *Rhetorical Career*, p. 38.

9. Hammerback and Jensen, *Rhetorical Career*, p. 83.

10. Hammerback and Jensen, *Rhetorical Career*, p. 134.

11. Hammerback and Jensen, *Rhetorical Career*, p. 140.

12. "Thanksgiving Message," *El Malcriado*, December 2, 1968, p. 7.

13. César Chávez, "The Mexican-American and the Church," in F. Chris García, ed., *La Causa Politica: A Chicano Political Reader* (Notre Dame: Uni-

versity of Notre Dame Press, 1974), p. 143; first published in *El Grito*, I, no. 4 (Summer 1968), pp. 9–12.

14. "Quotable Chavez," *Cleveland Press*, May 3, 1975.
15. "Quotable Chavez."
16. *National Catholic Reporter*, March 14, 1982.
17. *National Catholic Reporter*, March 14, 1982.
18. Levy, *Cesar Chavez*, p. 163.
19. Dalton, *Moral Vision*, p. 114.
20. Dalton, *Moral Vision*, p. 80.
21. Dalton, *Moral Vision*, p. 81.
22. Dalton, *Moral Vision*, pp. 81–82.
23. César Chávez to Dear Sister and Brother, March 10, 1970 in Anne Draper Collection, Box 4, Fld. 2 in Special Collections, Green Library, Stanford University.

César Chávez, 1970. Denver Public Library, Western History Collection.

CHAPTER FIVE

∽

Self-Sacrifice

But to bring dignity and empowerment to the poor, César Chávez also understood that sacrifice would be needed. Based on his faith and on the life of Jesus, César dedicated his life to self-sacrifice. He believed, as did St. Francis, that only by giving of yourself do you receive. He understood that only by giving of your life do you find life. César in his struggles did not sacrifice just for the sake of sacrifice, but because he sincerely believed that that was the most noble thing for humans to do. His whole life, as his own mother had taught him, was to help others, especially those in need. He epitomized this through his work with the farm workers. In the end, César sacrificed his own life for others and for their liberation. He reminded us through his own life that as humans our humanity is or should be judged by what we give to others, not what we give to ourselves. In the following quotes, César used the prefeminist term "man" to represent "mankind," but without question to also include women.

***

"When we are really honest with ourselves, we must admit that our lives are all that really belong to us. So it is how we use our lives that determines what kind of men we are. It is my deepest belief that only by giving our lives do we find life. I am convinced that the truest act of courage, the strongest act of manliness is to sacrifice ourselves for others in a totally nonviolent struggle for justice. To be a man is to suffer for others. God help us to be men."[1]

"We are working toward creating the new man, the new man in the fields, the man who will think of the common good, as you and I do, instead of the man who thinks of himself first."[2]

[In San Jose, during the 1950s people would go to César, as a member of the Community Service Organization (CSO), with various problems:]

"Since I had the inclination and the training, helping people came naturally. I wasn't thinking in terms of organizing members, but just a duty I had to do. That goes back to my mother's training. It was not until later that I realized that this was a good organizing tool, although maybe unconsciously, I was already beginning to understand."[3]

"Before the Farm Workers Union we had only each other to care for. It was our common problems and our common suffering that gave birth to this union, our own union, the Farm Workers Union. All around us were those who said it could never be done. Everywhere people said that the growers were too strong for us, that the police would be against us, that the courts would beat us down, and that sooner or later we would fall back into the poverty and despair of our forefathers. But we fooled them. We fooled them because our common suffering and our love for each other and our families kept us together and kept us sacrificing and fighting for the better tomorrow that all of us dream about as we work among the vines."[4]

"The problem is that some outsiders cannot understand the rewards of our way of life. They think we want to get out of it. It is a beautiful sight to watch things ripen, to have a feeling for what the land gives you if you are patient with it."[5]

"On behalf of the men and women of the farm worker movement, I am honored to join you in prayer during this Good Friday Service for

World Peace. Our prayer on this Good Friday 1986 is simple: we pray that Christians of every culture and class will seek to follow Jesus in the path that led him to the cross . . . that we will, each in our own place, make those everyday sacrifices for the poor, homeless and oppressed that can bring justice to our communities and peace to the world."[6]

"I would like people to choose one important area of human need and focus their energies in that direction—so much so that their lives are touched and changed by the people they work with. People should not be hesitant to give themselves to others or to a good cause. They should not fear the unknown or commitments that might change the way they have organized their lives. Let us go forth to find a new and fuller and happier life—I think a life closer to God. I guess that is one of my goals—to be closer to God."[7]

[From the Plan de Delano, 1966, Chávez's and the farm workers' declaration of independence:]
    "This is the beginning of a social movement in fact and not in pronouncement. We seek our basic, God-given rights as human beings. Because we have suffered, and are not afraid to suffer in order to survive, we are ready to give up everything—even our lives—in our struggle for social justice. We shall do it without violence because it is our destiny. To the growers and to all those who oppose us, we say the words of Benito Juárez [one of Mexico's greatest leaders of the nineteenth century], 'Respect for another's rights is the meaning of peace.'"[8]

[César Chávez at the funeral of farm worker Juan de la Cruz, August 21, 1973:]
    "Juan has not only given himself in life, but he has now given his only life on this earth for us, for his children and for all farm workers who suffer and who go hungry in this land of plenty.
    We are here because his spirit of service and sacrifice has touched and moved our lives. The force that is generated by that spirit of love is more powerful than any force on earth. It cannot be stopped."[9]

"Our job . . . is to educate our members so that they will be conscious of the needs of others less fortunate than themselves. The scope of the worker's interest must motivate him to reach out and help others. If we can get across the idea of participating in other causes, then we have real education."[10]

"Our people are ready to accept sacrifices. They have made many sacrifices in the decades of exploitation and humiliation they have faced as agricultural workers. They are ready to undergo more sacrifices in the course of their liberation. A year after the strike began, our people were willing to march 300 miles to Sacramento in order to witness to the validity and justice of their cause. In addition to this, the strikers have been willing to live without wages. The union only takes care of their basic needs, such as, rent, clothing, and food. Once people are willing to make these sacrifices, you develop a power of the spirit which can affect your adversaries in ways you can hardly imagine. Gandhi called this power 'moral jujitsu.'"[11]

"Ninety-five percent of the strikers lost their homes and cars. But I think that, in losing their worldly possessions in order to serve the poor, they found themselves."[12]

"He [Gandhi] believed that truth was vindicated, not by infliction of suffering on the opponent, but on oneself. That belief comes from Christ himself, the Sermon on the Mount, and further back from Jewish and Hindu traditions. There's no question that by setting such an example, you get others to do it. That is the real essence, but that is difficult. That's what separates ordinary men from great men. And we're all pretty ordinary men."[13]

"When you sacrifice, you force others to do the same. It is a powerful weapon. When someone stops eating for a week or 10 days, people come and want to be part of the experience. Those who are willing to sacrifice and be of service have little difficulty with people. When you work and sacrifice more than anyone around you, others feel the need to do at least a little bit more than they were doing before."[14]

"People are willing to make sacrifices. That is why our union is strong. Because the root of the union is sacrifice. Once we understand this, we can look years back and see that for many years we've had the idea of sacrificing ourselves to obtain something good for us and for our people. That is why, my fellow people, that I ask you for one last sacrifice, a big sacrifice that will take you to victory, a work sacrifice, a sacrifice to do it without violence, a sacrifice to work hard, and . . . to arrive at the final victory that is about to come."[15]

"Individuals have to decide to give their lives over to the struggle for specific and meaningful social change . . . their sacrifice and their suffering into a powerful campaign for dignity and for justice."[16]

"Perhaps we can bring the day when children will learn from their earliest days that being fully men and fully women means to give one's life to the liberation of the brother who suffers. It is up to each one of us. It won't happen unless we decide to use our own lives to show the way."[17]

"[I]n giving of yourself you will discover a whole new life of meaning and love."[18]

"Without the element of risk, I would be hypocritical. The whole essence of penance—which I'm a fool for because I think it works— would be taken away."[19]

"Our struggle is not easy. Those who oppose our cause are rich and powerful, and they have many allies in high places. We are poor. Our allies are few. But we have something the rich do not own. We have our own bodies and spirits and the justice of our cause as our weapons."[20]

[In 1970 at the end of the grape strike:]
    "The strikers and the people involved in the struggle sacrificed a lot, sacrificed all of their worldly possessions. . . . [T]hey found that only through dedication, through serving mankind, and, in this case, serving the poor and those who were struggling for justice, only in that way could they really find themselves."[21]

"[I]f we make democracy work, I'm convinced that's by far the best system. And it will work if people want it to. But to make it work for the poor, we have to work at it full time. And we have to be willing to just give up everything and risk it all."[22]

"If you're outraged at conditions then you can't possibly be free or happy until you devote all your time to changing them and do nothing but that. . . . But you can't change anything if you want to hold onto a good job, a good way of life, and avoid sacrifice."[23]

"I have to give up a lot of things, because I can't ask people to sacrifice if I won't sacrifice myself."[24]

"No one accepts death, I think, but what is the alternative? If you lock yourself in or give up, it's a living death; that's no alternative. Death is not enough to stop you. You're really too busy to think of it. Unimportant, day-to-day things get your attention, which is just as well."[25]

"It all comes down to the question of what we are going to do on earth. Are we here to make money? Are we here just to get what we can for ourselves? Or are we here to do something for our brothers? You really can't help people unless you are willing to sacrifice yourself because first there are always greater demands upon your time than you can take care of and second, everything you do becomes controversial. So you have these attacks against you all the time. That is the sacrifice. If you are not prepared for those two things you cannot help people because you cannot take the pressure. So it seems to me that if one understands that it is part of the sacrifice, then you can take it, live with it, and even sometimes accept it."[26]

"We began to do away with a lot of little things we thought we just had to have, things we really did not need. We begin to get that commitment, that gut commitment—this sacrifice won't be for nothing. I made it for six months, nothing will stop me now."[27]

[During the grape strike against Schenley Industries in April 1966, Chávez stated:]

"But without the courage and desire to win on part of the workers, our victory over Schenley would never have been possible. Their willingness to suffer has made their victory possible."[28]

"[T]he real saints today are [union organizers, who work for five dollars a week and premiums]. They are doing what Christ said—caring for their brothers."[29]

[César spoke the following words after the death of nineteen farm workers in a bus crash in 1974:]

"But brothers and sisters, the men and women we honor here today are important human beings. They are important because they are from us. We cherish them. We love them. We will miss them. They are important because of the love they gave to their husbands, their children, their wives, their parents—all those who were close to them and who needed them. They are important because of the work they do. They are not implements to be used and discarded. They are human beings who sweat and sacrifice to bring food to the tables of millions and millions of people throughout the world. They are important because God made them, gave them life, and cares for them in life and in death."[30]

"We seek our basic, God-given rights as human beings. Because we have suffered—and are not afraid to suffer—in order to survive, we are ready to give up everything, even our lives, in our fight for justice."[31]

"What keeps me going? Well, it's like a fire—a consuming, nagging everyday and every-moment demand of my soul to just do it. It's difficult to explain. I like to think it's the good Spirit asking me to do it. I hope so. . . . If you really want something, you have to sacrifice. Because of my faith the concept of sacrifice is understood."[32]

"My mother always insisted that we share with people even when we kids objected because we were hungry ourselves. So I grew up with a very special feeling about the suffering of farm workers and with this faith that I received from my family and from the Church. It came naturally to us to hope for the future and to want to make things better in the world. It seemed so obvious that God wanted more equality and more justice, and that God expected people to work for these things."[33]

"Those who are willing to sacrifice and be of service have very little difficulty with people. They know what they are all about. People can't help
but want to be near them—to help them and work with them. That's
what love is all about. It starts with you and radiates out. You can't phony
it. It just doesn't go. When you work and sacrifice more than anyone else
around you, you put others on the spot and they have to do at least a bit
more than they've been doing. And that's what puts it together."[34]

"We know that we have a commitment to help people as we've been
helped. We'll never lose that. And that's the promise we make you
right here today."[35]

"Nan Freeman and Sal Santos have given their lives for our movement
this past year. They were very young. It hurt us to lose them, and it still
hurts us. But the greatest tragedy is not to live and die, as we all must.
The greatest tragedy is for a person to live and die without knowing the
satisfaction of giving life for others. The greatest tragedy is to be born
but not to live for fear of losing a little security or because we are afraid
of loving and giving ourselves to other people."[36]

"We are here today to say that true wealth is not measured in money or
status or power. It is measured in the legacy we leave behind for those
we love and those we inspire. We are here today because our lives were
touched and moved by her spirit of love and service. That spirit is more
powerful than any force on earth. It cannot be stopped."[37]

"Our cause goes on in hundreds of distant places. It multiplies among
thousands and then millions of caring people who heed through a multitude of simple deeds the commandment set out in the book of the
Prophet Micah, in the Old Testament: 'What does the Lord require of
you, but to do justice, to love kindness, and to walk humbly with your
God.'"[38]

"[U]nity means that we must make sacrifices, but these are necessary to
sustain the life of the whole organization; they are essential. When we
decide on the goal of a particular work, it is necessary to hold on to it,
not only with our lips, but always actively; it is necessary for this goal

to become a rule of life. He who knows principles is not equal to he who loves them."[39]

"I like the whole idea of sacrifice to do things. If they are done that way, they are more lasting. If they cost more, then we will value them more."[40]

"It is a question of suffering with some kind of hope. That's better than suffering with no hope at all."[41]

"Justice not Charity
Dignity not Mercy
Servant hood, not Service"[42]

"The job can't be done unless there is a commitment. If we're going to lead people and ask them to starve and really sacrifice, we've got to do it first, do it more than anybody else, because it isn't the orders, it isn't the pronouncements, it's the deeds that count."[43]

"We are weak. And the weak have no rights, but [only] the right to sacrifice until they are strong."[44]

"We'll organize workers as long as we're willing to sacrifice."[45]

"It is my deepest belief that only by giving our lives do we find life."[46]

Notes

1. Jacques Levy, *Cesar Chavez: Autobiography of La Causa* (New York: W. W. Norton & Company, 1975), p. 286.

2. John C. Hammerback and Richard J. Jensen, *The Rhetorical Career of César Chávez* (College Station: Texas A & M Press, 1998), p. 106.

3. Levy, *Cesar Chavez*, pp. 110–111.

4. Richard J. Jensen and John C. Hammerback, eds., *The Words of César Chávez* (College Station: Texas A & M Press, 2002), pp. 78–79.

5. "Quotable Chavez," *Cleveland Press*, May 3, 1975.

6. Chávez statement, no source cited.

7. *Visitor*, November 30, 1980.

8. Hammerback and Jensen, *Rhetorical Career*, p. 80.

9. Jensen and Hammerback, *Words of César Chávez*, p. 181.

10. Chávez, "Introduction," in Mark Day, *Forty Acres: Cesar Chavez and the Farm Workers* (New York: Praeger Publishers, 1971), p. 10.

11. Day, *Forty Acres*, p. 115.

12. Day, *Forty Acres*, p. 167.

13. Levy, *Cesar Chavez*, p. 92.

14. "Farm Union is Alive," *Los Angeles Times*, January 2, 1975, p. 7.

15. Hammerback and Jensen, *Rhetorical Career*, p. 73.

16. Hammerback and Jensen, *Rhetorical Career*, pp. 106–107.

17. Hammerback and Jensen, *Rhetorical Career*, p. 107.

18. Hammerback and Jensen, *Rhetorical Career*, p. 108.

19. Levy, *Cesar Chavez*, p. 285.

20. Levy, *Cesar Chavez*, p. 286.

21. Levy, *Cesar Chavez*, p. 325.

22. Levy, *Cesar Chavez*, p. 538.

23. Hammerback and Jensen, *Rhetorical Career*, p. 21.

24. Peter Matthiessen, *Sal Si Puedes: Cesar Chavez and the New American Revolution* (New York: Random House, 1969), p. 25.

25. Matthiessen, *Sal Si Puedes*, p. 199.

26. Ronald B. Taylor, *Chavez and the Farm Workers* (Boston: Beacon Press, 1975), p. 139.

27. Levy, *Cesar Chavez*, p. 5.

28. "Farm Union Gets Recognition," *National Catholic Reporter*, April 13, 1966, p. 1.

29. "Rendering Unto César," *Christianity Today*, July 3, 1970, p. 32.

30. Frederick John Dalton, *The Moral Vision of César Chávez* (Maryknoll, NY: Orbis Books, 2003), p. 9.

31. Dalton, *Moral Vision.*, p. 88.

32. Dalton, *Moral Vision*, p. 162.

33. Dalton, *Moral Vision*, p. 162.

34. Jensen and Hammerback, *Words of César Chávez*, p. 71.

35. Jensen and Hammerback, *Words of César Chávez*, p. 85.

36. Jensen and Hammerback, *Words of César Chávez*, p. 168.

37. Jensen and Hammerback, *Words of César Chávez*, p. 172.

38. Jensen and Hammerback, *Words of César Chávez*, p. 150.

39. Winthrop Yinger, *Cesar Chavez: The Rhetoric of Nonviolence* (Hicksville, NY: Exposition Press, 1975), p. 103.

40. Levy, *Cesar Chavez*, pp. 92–93.

41. Luis A. Solis-Garza, "César Chávez: The Chicano 'Messiah?'" in Edward Simmen, *Pain and Promise: The Chicano Today* (New York: New American Library, 1972), p. 304.

42. Hammerback and Jensen, *Rhetorical Career*, p. 154.

43. Richard Griswold del Castillo and Richard A. García, *César Chávez: A Triumph of Spirit* (Norman: University of Oklahoma Press, 1995), p. 56.

44. Griswold del Castillo and García, *César Chávez*, p. 154.

45. Jane Marie Yett, "Farm Labor Struggles in California, 1970–1973, In Light of Reinhold Niebuhr's Concepts of Power and Justice," unpublished Ph.D. dissertation, Graduate Theological Union, Berkeley, 1980, p. 152.

46. Yinger, *Cesar Chavez*, p. 75.

CHAPTER SIX

~

Nonviolence

Influenced by his parents, by his own nature, and by his knowledge of Gandhi, and inspired by Dr. Martin Luther King, Jr., César Chávez embraced the concept of nonviolence. His struggle with the farm workers was centered on nonviolence. César understood that given the power of the growers and their access to police forces, the employment of violent tactics by the workers would be self-defeating. But nonviolence was more than a strategy, as César often pointed out. It was recognition of the value of human life. Those who did not recognize the humanity of others only carried out violence. César's Catholic principles would not lead him down this path. Because he believed in the human dignity of every individual and the sanctity of life, he embraced nonviolence as a way of life and as part of his spirituality. At the same time, César understood that nonviolence was not easy and that it was a process. You had to work hard to be nonviolent. He admitted that he was a violent man striving to be nonviolent. Yet nonviolence did not suggest passivity. César called for "militant nonviolence." By this he meant that nonviolence involved struggle and the use of pressure to achieve the goals of the farm workers, but in a nonviolent manner. Through this approach and through the efforts of the farm workers, César Chávez became one of the great champions of nonviolence and peace.

***

"I am not a nonviolent man. I am a violent man who is trying to be nonviolent."[1]

"When I read the biography of St. Francis of Assisi, I was moved when he went before the Moslem prince and offered to walk through fire to end a bloody war. And I still remember how he talked and made friends with a wolf that had killed several men. St. Francis was a gentle and humble man."[2]

"In the St. Francis biography, there was a reference to Gandhi and others who practiced nonviolence. That was a theme that struck a very responsive chord, probably because of the foundation laid by my mother. So the next thing I read after St. Francis was the Louis Fischer biography of Gandhi."[3]

"Gandhi described his tactics as moral jujitsu—always hitting the opposition off-balance, but keeping his principles. His tactics of civil disobedience haven't hit this country on a massive scale, but they will. Anybody who comes out with the right way of doing it is going to throw the government into a real uproar. If they have a good issue, and they find a good vehicle for civil disobedience, they're going to be devastating."[4]

"155 years ago [on September 16, 1810] in the state of Guanajuato in Mexico a padre [Fr. Miguel Hidalgo] proclaimed the struggle for liberty. He was killed, but ten years later Mexico won its independence. . . . We engaged in another struggle for the freedom and dignity which poverty denies us. But it must not be a violent struggle, even if violence is used against us. Violence can only hurt us and our cause."[5]

[After the grape strike started in fall 1965:]
"The growers were giving us the knee and the elbow, knocking us down and throwing us down. But we remained nonviolent. We weren't afraid of them. We just got up and continued picketing."[6]

"It's so hard to maintain a nonviolent approach to doing things, but within our Union, we are still succeeding. . . . Nonviolence has one big demand, the need to be creative, and the ideas come from the people. . . . If someone commits violence against us, it is much better—if we can—not to react against the violence, but to react in such a way as to get closer to our goal. People don't like to see a nonviolent movement subjected to violence, and there's a lot of support across the country for nonviolence. That's the key point we have going for us. We can turn the world if we can do it nonviolently. So, if we can just show people how they can organize nonviolently, we can't fail. It has never failed when it's been tried. If the effort gets out of hand, it's from lack of discipline."[7]

"To us the boycott of grapes was the most near-perfect of nonviolent struggles, because nonviolence also requires mass involvement. The boycott demonstrated to the whole country, the whole world, what people can do by nonviolent action."[8]

"[A] supermarket boycott is an effective nonviolent weapon. Fire is not. When a fire destroys a supermarket, the company collects the insurance and rebuilds the store bigger and better, and also marks off the loss in its income tax. But picket lines take away customers and reduce business, and there is no way for the store to compensate for that. It is driven by sheer economics to want to avoid picket lines."[9]

"Nonviolence in the abstract is a very difficult thing to comprehend or explain. I'd read a lot, but all of it was in the abstract. It's difficult to carry the message to people who aren't involved. Nonviolence must be placed in context."[10]

"People equate nonviolence with inaction—with not doing anything—and it's not that at all. It's exactly the opposite."[11]

"Gandhi never said not to do anything. He said exactly the opposite. He said, 'Do something! Offer your life!' He said, 'If you really want to do something, be willing to die for it.' That's asking for the maximum contribution."[12]

"Nonviolence is action. Like anything else, though, it's got to be organized. There must be rules. There must be people following."[13]

"Naturally, nonviolence takes time. But poverty has been with us since the beginning of time. We just have to work for improvement. I despise exploitation and I want change, but I'm willing to pay the price in terms of time. There's a Mexican saying, 'Hay más tiempo que vida'— There's more time than life. We've got all the time in the world."[14]

"Some great nonviolent successes have been achieved in history. Moses is about the best example, and the first one. Christ also is a beautiful example, as is the way the Christians overcame tyranny. They needed over three hundred years, but they did it. The most recent example is Gandhi. To me that's the most beautiful one. We can examine it more closely because it happened during our lifetime. It's fantastic how he got so many people to do things, which is the whole essence of nonviolent action."[15]

"First, of course, the workers have to understand nonviolence. Gandhi once said he'd rather have a man be violent than be a coward. I agree. If he's a coward, then what good is he for anyone? But it is our job to see he's not a coward. That's really the beginning point of our training."[16]

"And while the philosophy of nonviolence covers physical, verbal, and moral behaviors, we haven't achieved that goal. If we can achieve it, we're saints—which we're not. We're still working on eliminating physical violence, though that isn't all. . . . After workers begin to understand physical nonviolence among people, then we also apply it to property and go on from there."[17]

"Nonviolence becomes more powerful as nonviolence becomes more pronounced."[18]

"We shouldn't get mad, because then we might do something not consistent with our philosophy of nonviolence, and we have many nonviolent means at our disposal."[19]

"[T]hrough nonviolent action in this nation and across the world . . . social justice can be gotten."[20]

"[T]o be nonviolent in a monastery is one thing, but being nonviolent in a struggle for justice is another."[21]

"You reap what you sow; if we become violent with others, then we will become violent among ourselves. Social justice for the dignity of man cannot be won at the price of human life. You cannot justify what you want for La Raza, for the people, and in the same breath destroy one life. . . . I will not compromise. Racism is wrong, racism is not the way, nationalism is not the way."[22]

"Knowing of Gandhi's admonition that fasting is the last resort in place of the sword, during a most critical time in our movement last February [1968], I undertook a 25-day fast. I repeat to you the principle enunciated to the membership at the start of the fast: If to build our union required the deliberate taking of life, either the life of a grower or his child or the life of a farm worker or his child then I would choose not to see the union built. We advocate militant nonviolence as our means for social revolution and to achieve justice for our people, but we are not blind or deaf to the desperate and moody winds of human frustration, impatience, and rage that blow among us. . . . Men are not angels and the time and tides wait for no man. Precisely because of these powerful human emotions, we have tried to involve the mass of people in their own struggle. Participation and self-determination remain the best experience of freedom; and free men instinctively prefer democratic change . . . only the enslaved in despair have need of violent overthrow. . . . We hate the agribusiness system that seeks to keep us enslaved, and we shall overcome and change it not by retaliation or bloodshed, but by a determined nonviolent struggle carried on by those masses of farm workers who intend to be free and human."[23]

"[The] issue becomes how you go about your work, violent or nonviolent. It takes a lot not to strike back. . . . The reaction, I guess, is built in us. But if you really understand what it is you are doing, not only being willing to give up your time to help solve an injustice, but also be willing to take all of the abuse that comes with it, and on top of that understand that it has to be done nonviolently, then I think you understand the character of nonviolence."[24]

"Truth needs another element, and that is time. If you have those two elements, truth and time, and you understand them, then there is no reason why anyone would want to be violent. Number one, sooner or later truth is going to be exposed. It cannot be hidden, you know? Mankind has never been able to deal with the suppression of truth."[25]

"If you understand what time means—and I am speaking of time in terms of not what you have here, today, but in terms of [if] you . . . lose a strike . . . you haven't lost anything. The loss is a temporary condition. As long as you know this, the only thing you have lost is a tiny bit of time, not the main strike itself—if you understand time in these terms then violence is not really that important. Violence really doesn't win anything for you in the long run. So you see, what I am really talking about is the common sense of nonviolence."[26]

"I am often asked if our youth, especially the young Mexican Americans, will choose the way of nonviolence to make the necessary changes in our society. I don't think that violence will be a way of life for any significant number of people. Although many may espouse the rhetoric of violence, few will physically commit violence. Meanwhile, we must be vitally concerned about educating people to the significance of peace and nonviolence as positive forces in our society. . . . We are concerned with peace, because violence (and war is the worst type of violence) has no place in our society or in our world, and it must be eradicated. Next to union contracts, we must focus our attention to bring about the necessary changes in our society through nonviolent means. We must train effective organizers for this purpose. We must acquaint people with peace—not because capitalism is better or communism is better, but because, as men, we are better. As men we don't want to kill anyone, and we don't want to be killed ourselves. We must reach everyone so that this message can go out. If we do this correctly, our people will rise above mere material interests and goods. They will become involved in cultural matters. And we need a cultural revolution among ourselves—not only in art but also in the realm of the spirit. As poor people and immigrants, all of us have brought to this country some very important things of the spirit. But too often they are choked, they are not allowed to flourish in our society."[27]

"I undertook this Fast [1968] because my heart was filled with grief and pain for the suffering of farm workers. The Fast was first for me and then for all of us in this Union. It was a Fast for nonviolence and a call to sacrifice."[28]

"I think nonviolence is a new natural way of doing things, and violence is highly out of the ordinary."[29]

"Nonviolence exacts a very high price from one who practices it. But once you are able to meet that demand then you can do most things, provided you have the time. Gandhi showed how a whole nation could be liberated without an army. This is the first time in the history of the world when a huge nation, occupied for over a century, achieved independence by nonviolence. It was a long struggle and it takes time."[30]

"I am firmly convinced that nonviolence cannot exist only in books or on the seminar level on our university campuses, but it must exist in the flesh. I have always believed that people are the most important element we have. We must put flesh into our nonviolence rather than simply talk about it."[31]

"If we can just show people how they can organize nonviolently, we can't fail. It has never failed where it's been tried. If the effort gets out of hand, it's from a lack of discipline."[32]

"Nonviolence is more powerful than violence. We are convinced that nonviolence supports you if you have a just and moral cause. Nonviolence gives the opportunity to stay on the offensive, which is of vital importance to win any contest."[33]

"[T]rue nonviolence is an impossibility without the possession of unadulterated fearlessness."[34]

"There is no such thing as defeat in nonviolence [that does not depend on] the good will of the oppressor, but rather on the unfailing assistance of God."[35]

"In nonviolence the cause has to be just and clear as well as the means."[36]

"You have to train to be nonviolent just as a soldier trains to be violent. Nonviolence is people willing to reject violence and say, 'Okay, there's another way of doing it.' That way entails love, sacrifice, lots of work, some planning, and getting a real satisfaction from doing it."[37]

"When we win isn't important. The rich have money—and the poor have time. We don't have to win this year or next year or even the year after that. We'll just keep plugging away, day after day, until the boycott takes its toll. We will never give up. We have nothing else to do with our lives except to continue in this nonviolent fight."[38]

"Nonviolence means that masses of people come to the aid of their less fortunate brothers who are legally, legitimately, and nonviolently trying to get a better life for themselves and their families."[39]

"Nonviolence is not cowardice. A nonviolent person cannot be fearful. He must be on his toes at all times. He must be a strategist. He must know how to deal with people, above all. You see, nonviolence means that you involve people in creative ways. The real force of nonviolence is in the numbers."[40]

"No leader is violent by nature. Very often violence is used by an individual in order to overthrow another leader. It is used like a tool. It is in vogue now. But, deep down in their hearts, these people do not really believe in violence."[41]

"In order to build a successful nonviolent movement, you must be involved in it night and day. You must be occupied with it constantly. You must do nothing more and nothing less than the movement. Nonviolence depends on the absolute loyalty of the leadership to their cause, and the ability of the leadership to attract and organize other people."[42]

[Statement released by César Chávez from the Monterey County Jail, December 5, 1970:]

"I'm in good spirits, and they're very kind to me. I was spiritually prepared for this confinement. I don't think the judge was unfair. I am prepared to pay the price for civil disobedience. I am still very committed and I'm not bitter at all. At this point in our struggle there is more need than ever to demonstrate our love for those who oppose us. Farm workers are wounded every day by being denied representation of the union of their choice. Jail is a small price to pay to help right that injustice."[43]

"Nonviolence is a very powerful weapon. Most people don't understand the power of nonviolence and tend to be angered by the whole idea. Those who have been nonviolent in bringing about change and see the difference between violence and nonviolence are firmly committed to a lifetime of nonviolence, not because it's easy or because it is cowardly, but because it is an effective and very powerful way. Nonviolence means people in action. People have to understand that with nonviolence goes a hell of a lot of organization."[44]

"[In] seeking social change, I am positive nonviolence is the way, morally and tactically, especially in our society where those in power resort to clubs, tear gas, and guns. I have seen nonviolence work many times in many ways. When we organized California's vineyards, for example, it was the growers' violence, their manipulation of the police and the courts, that helped gain support for our cause."[45]

"We can remain nonviolent because people outside the Movement by and large don't want violence. By remaining nonviolent in the face of violence, we win them to our side, and that's what makes the strength. And we organize that strength to fight for change."[46]

"The first day we took a vote to strike I asked for a nonviolent vote. I have been asked this question [why are you an advocate of nonviolence?] many times and I have really had to dig back and find out. I think it goes back to my family, particularly my mother. She's a very illiterate participant. She never learned how to read or write, never learned English, never went to school for a day. She has this natural childishness about how to live, and how to let people live. In the old days, at least when I was a kid—it was generally true in a lot of families, much less so now in my family—there were occasions when she would gather us around her and she would call it *consejo*. 'Consejo' means to council [sic] to advise, she didn't wait until it would happen—like: 'You fight now? Well here it comes! I'm going to tell you how bad it is to fight!' I remember that she would talk constantly about nonviolence—constantly."[47]

"We are engaged in another struggle for the freedom and dignity which poverty denies us. But it must not be a violent struggle, even if violence is used against us. Violence can only hurt us and our cause."[48]

"I've done a little tracing—not only my mother but both sides—and our people were very peaceful on both sides. We didn't have any generals or warriors. Very plain peons, so I think that's where it started. My Dad never fought. We never saw my Dad fight or drink or smoke—all the things that have a bad meaning."[49]

"I think nonviolence is a very natural way of doing things, and violence is highly out of the ordinary."[50]

"We advocate militant nonviolence as our means of achieving justice for our people, but we are not blind to the feelings of frustration, impatience and anger which seethe inside every farm worker. The burden of generations of poverty and powerlessness lies . . . in the fields of California. If we fail, there are those who will see revenge and violence as the shortcut to change. It is to overcome these powerful human emotions that we have involved, through the strike and boycott, masses of people in their own struggle. Freedom is best expressed through participation and self-determination, and free men and women instinctively prefer democratic change to any other means. Thus, the strike and boycott are not only weapons against the growers, but our way of avoiding the senseless violence, that brings no honor to any class or neighborhood. For, nonviolence is more than academic theory; it is the very lifeblood of our movement."[51]

"We took every case of violence and publicized what they were doing to us. By some strange chemistry, every time the opposition commits an unjust act against our hopes and aspirations, we get tenfold paid back in benefits."[52]

"We must respect all human life, in the cities and in the fields and in Vietnam. Nonviolence is the only weapon that is compassionate and recognizes each man's value. We want to preserve that value in our enemies—or in our adversaries, as President Kennedy said more gently, more rightly. We want to protect the victim from being the victim. We want to protect the executioner from being the executioner."[53]

"How in the hell can you get a theologian to accept that one or two or three lives are worth giving up for some material gain? It doesn't stop there, it is just the beginning. The real paradox here is that the people who advocate peace in Vietnam advocate violence in their country. Inconceivable; I don't understand it."[54]

[Telegram from César Chávez to Mrs. Martin Luther King, Jr., El Malcriado, April 15, 1968, p. 5:]
    "We are deeply saddened to learn of the death of your husband. Our prayers are for you and your children in your sorrow. It is my belief that much of the courage which we have found in our struggle for justice in the fields has had its roots in the example set by your husband and by those multitudes who fueled his nonviolent leadership. We owe so much to Dr. Martin Luther King, the words alone cannot express our gratefulness. Despite the tragic violence which took your husband, there is much that is good about our nation. It was to that goodness that your husband appealed. It was that compassion in all of us that he reached out to touch. His nonviolence was that of action—not that of one contemplating action. Because of that, he will always be to us more than a philosopher of nonviolence, rather he will be remembered by us as a man of peace."[55]

"It has been our experience that few men or women ever have the opportunity to know the true satisfaction that comes with giving one's life totally in the nonviolent struggle for justice. Martin Luther King, Jr., was one of these unique servants and from him we learned many of the lessons that have guided us. For these lessons and for his sacrifice for the poor and oppressed, Dr. King's memory will be cherished in the hearts of the farm workers forever."[56]

[In the grape strike against DiGiorgio Corporation in 1966, the farm workers were prohibited from picketing due to a court injunction. Some of the farm worker women suggested that instead of picketing, a prayer vigil be commenced:]

"I got Richard [César's brother] and had him take my old station wagon and build a little chapel on it. It was like a shrine with a picture of Our Lady of Guadalupe, some candles, and some flowers. We worked on it until about 2:00 in the morning. Then we parked it across from the DiGiorgio gate where we started a vigil that lasted two months. People were there day and night. The next morning we distributed a leaflet all the way from Bakersfield to Visalia inviting people to a prayer meeting at the DiGiorgio Ranch and made the same announcement on the Spanish radio. People came by the hundreds. You could see cars two miles in either direction. . . .

[Next day] The same evening about fifty women came. The next evening, half of the camp was out, and from then on, every single day, they were out there. Every day we had a mass, held a meeting, sang spirituals, and got them to sign authorization cards. These meetings were responsible in large part for keeping the spirit up of our people inside the camps and helping our organizing for the coming battle. It was a beautiful demonstration of the power of nonviolence."[57]

"We live in the midst of people who hate and fear us. They have worked hard to keep us in our place. They will spend millions more to destroy our union. But we do not have to make ourselves small by hating and fearing them in return. There is enough love and goodwill in our movement to give energy to our struggle and still have plenty left over to break down and change the climate of hate and fear around us."[58]

"We are . . . convinced that nonviolence is more powerful than violence. Nonviolence supports you if you have a just and moral course.

Nonviolence provides the opportunity to stay on the offensive, and that is of crucial importance to win any contest."[59]

"[I]f we are committed to nonviolence only as a strategy or tactics, then if it fails our only alternative is to turn to violence. So we must balance the strategy with a clear understanding of what we are doing. However important the struggle is and however much misery, poverty and exploitation exist, we know that it cannot be more important than one human life. We work on the theory that men and women who are truly concerned about people are nonviolent by nature."[60]

"The grower will use many tricks to make us violate the law through violence. But it will not be done. Growers will accuse us of breaking the law (and this is why: Because they make the law), but we will never use violence against a person or a person's property because that is not our destiny."[61]

"Their [farm workers'] nonviolent struggle is not soft or easy. It requires hard work and discipline more than anything else. It means giving up on economic security. It requires patience and determination. Farm workers are working to build a nonviolent army trained and ready to sacrifice in order to change conditions for all of our brothers in the fields."[62]

"It is now clear to me that the war in Vietnam is gutting the soul of our nation. Of course we know the war to be wrong and unjustifiable, but today we see it has destroyed the moral fiber of the people. Our resistance to this, and all wars, stems from a deep faith in nonviolence. We have to acknowledge that violent warfare between opposing groups—be it over issues of labor or race—is not justifiable. Violence is like acid—it corrodes the movement's dedication to justice."[63]

"There is no such thing as means and ends. Everything we do is an end, in itself, that we can never erase. That is why we must make all our actions the kind we would like to be judged on, although they might be our last—which they might well be, who knows? That is why we will not let ourselves be provoked by our adversaries into behaving hatefully."[64]

"When a man or woman, young or old, takes a place on the picket line for even a day or two, he will never be the same again. He has confirmed his own humanity. Through nonviolence, he has confirmed the humanity of the others."[65]

"Gandhi taught that the boycott is the most nearly perfect instrument of nonviolent change, allowing masses of people to participate actively in a cause. It is in this sense that we make use of it. Even if people cannot picket with us or contribute money or food, they can take part in our struggle by not buying certain products. It is such a simple sacrifice to make."[66]

"Nonviolence can only be used by those whose cause is strong. It is very hard, and man's self control is very weak. I am not completely nonviolent yet, and I know it. That is why I fasted; I felt it was a very personal form of self-testing and of prayer. Anyone could be nonviolent in a monastery, after all, but that is easy and that was not the way of Christ. What's difficult is to be nonviolent in the cause, in the battle for social justice; knowing what violence can be done to ourselves, knowing—and this is even more difficult—what violence can be done to our family and brothers and our cause."[67]

"We had also read in the many attempts to organize workers that violence had played a large part in suppression of the union. We knew that the moment we struck that justice was going to be about 20 percent for us and 80 percent for the opposition. . . . So I asked the workers to take a vote to consider that this strike be a nonviolent strike. And many of them didn't know what nonviolent strike meant. But many of them did know that there was another group in the country that had been making a lot of progress for human rights and that was also committed to nonviolence, and this was the civil rights movement."[68]

"The more repression we get, the more solidified we get and the more we fight. It's an obvious fact. Because, you see, the more we get persecuted, the more martyrs there are. And that's the history of mankind. We are going to do it nonviolently—that's our destiny; we're committed to it. We're doing it nonviolently because we know the effects of nonviolence. We're doing it nonviolently because nonviolent action is superior to any type of action and more lasting. . . . We're going to do it that way because we [want] . . . to show other people who have grievances like here today, that nonviolent action has with it truth and has with it tremendous power that cannot be generated in any other way."[69]

"Our conviction is that human life is a very special possession given by God to man and that no one has the right to take it for any reason or for any cause, however just it may be. We are also convinced that non-violence is more powerful than violence. Nonviolence supports you if you have a just and moral cause. Nonviolence provides the opportunity to stay on the offensive, and that is of crucial importance to win any contest."[70]

"If we resort to violence then one of two things will happen: either the violence will be escalated and there will be many injuries and perhaps deaths on both sides, or there will be total demoralization of the workers. Nonviolence has exactly the opposite effect. If, for every violent act committed against us, we respond with nonviolence, we attract people's support. We can gather the support of millions who have a conscience and would rather see a nonviolent resolution to problems. We are convinced that when people are faced with a direct appeal from the poor struggling nonviolently against great odds, they will react positively. The American people and people everywhere still yearn for justice. It is to that yearning that we appeal."[71]

"It is possible to become discouraged about the injustice we see everywhere. But God did not promise us that the world would be humane and just. He gives us the gift of life and allows us to choose the way we will use our limited time on this earth. It is an awesome opportunity. We should be thankful for the life we have been given, thankful for the opportunity to do something about the suffering of our fellow man. We *can choose* to use our lives for others to bring about a better and more just world for our children. People who make that choice will know hardship and sacrifice. But if you give yourself totally to the nonviolent struggle for peace and justice, you also find that people will give you their hearts and that you will never go hungry and never be alone. And in giving of yourself you will discover a whole new life full of meaning and love."[72]

"If you have no basis for nonviolence other than a strategy, a tactic, then when it fails your only alternative is completely the reverse and that's violence. So you have to balance the strategy with a clear understanding of what you are doing. However important the struggle is and however much misery and poverty and degradation exist, we know that it cannot be more important than one human life. That's basic."[73]

"We operate on the theory that men who are involved and truly concerned about people are not by nature violent. If they were violent they couldn't have that love and that concern for people. That sort of man becomes violent when that deep concern he has for people is frustrated, when he's faced with overwhelming odds against what he is trying to do. Then sometimes he feels that violence is really a short cut or a sort of miracle to end everything and bring about a solution. We don't want to get into that trap."[74]

"If you use violence, you have to sell part of yourself for that violence, either because of your own self-guilt or because you have to incorporate people who are extremists and violent. . . . Then you are no longer the master of your own struggle, and the important thing is . . . for poor people to be able to get a clean victory, something you don't often see. If we get it through violence, then the employers will just wait long enough until they can get even with you—and then the workers will respond, and then. . . ."[75]

"If we were to become violent and we won the strike, as an example, then what would prevent us from turning violence against opponents in the movement who wanted to displace us? Say they felt they had more leadership and they wanted to be the leaders. What would prevent us from turning violence against them? Nothing. Because we had already experienced that violence awarded us victory. If we are concerned about human beings and if we are concerned about respecting man, then we have to be concerned about the consequences. Another thing is that people think nonviolence is really weak and non-militant.

These are misconceptions that people have because they don't under-stand what nonviolence means. Nonviolence takes more guts, if I can put it bluntly, than violence. Most violent acts are accomplished by getting the opponent off guard, and it doesn't take that much charac-ter, I think, if one wants to do it. I am confronted frequently by people who say, 'So and so tried nonviolence and it didn't work.' That's not re-ally so. Nonviolence is very weak in the theoretical sense; it cannot de-fend itself. But it is most powerful in the action situation where people are using nonviolence because they want desperately to bring about some change. Nonviolence in action is a very potent force and it can't be stopped. The people who are struggling have the complete say-so. No man-made law, no human ruler, no army can destroy this. There is no way it can be destroyed, except by those within the nonviolent struggle. And so, if we have the capacity to endure, if we have the pa-tience, things will change."[76]

"Nonviolence is essential to our work. And we cannot have others try to help us by being violent."[77]

"Nonviolence is very difficult. In our case our job is never done because we're always dealing with new people in these situations. We're always at the beginning point. Where you happen to deal with people you've dealt with before, it's no problem, but that's not afforded us very often. And so we now have 10,000 people on strike in seven different places and in almost every single case—with 98 percent of the people—they've never had the experience. That's difficult. You have to deal with them in such a way that you don't impose the idea of nonviolence on them but that they accept it. Because if you try to impose it in a sit-uation as difficult as this one, a situation that's so charged up, they'll re-ject everything. You have to have a very skilled method of convincing people. I think the first prerequisite of nonviolence is for the nonvio-lent person to assume that there are other feelings and not to impose. Trying to impose is a mistake a lot of nonactivist nonviolent people fall into, just as they fall into the trap of thinking nonviolence is a land of milk and honey. Nonviolence is really tough. You don't practice non-violence by attending conferences—you practice it on the picket lines. And if you've been here two or three days, you know how difficult that is. But once the workers make that first step toward nonviolence and they accept the idea, then you begin to work at carrying it out. It goes by steps. We're fortunate. We've been able to hang on to nonviolence in these really large confrontations we've been having. Some people still throw rocks—but they're not carrying guns or knives or baseball bats and the rock throwing is only occasional. So we think we're 99 and 9/10 percent successful."[78]

"The business of nonviolence in struggle is not angelic. It's the business of working with people—at best it's a very tough proposition."[79]

"With the struggle here, we'll sit back and we'll talk about nonviolence and we'll have made more converts than you'll ever make by going to ten million seminars. But also you'll have accomplished just what they want to accomplish. What do the poor care about strange philosophies of nonviolence if it doesn't mean bread for them? Right now . . . if people are not pacifists, it's not their fault. It's because society puts them in that spot. You've got to change it. You don't just change a man—you've got to change his environment as you do it."[80]

"Many people feel that an organization that uses nonviolent methods to reach victories must continue winning victories one after the other in order to remain nonviolent. If that be the case then a lot of efforts have been miserable failures. There is a great deal more involved than victories. My experience has been that the poor know violence more intimately than most people because it has been part of their lives, whether the violence of the gun or the violence of want and need."[81]

"I don't subscribe to the belief that nonviolence is cowardice as some militant groups are saying. In some instances nonviolence requires more militancy than violence. Nonviolence forces you to abandon the shortcut in trying to make a change in the racist order. Violence . . . is the trap people fall into when they begin to feel that it is the only way to act on their goal. When these people turn to violence it is a very savage kind."[82]

"I have just begun the seventh day of a personal fast of penance and hope. After so many months of struggle and slow progress, I have become fearful that our common commitment to nonviolence is weakening and that we may take dangerous shortcuts to victory. I accept full responsibility for this temptation and for all of its possible negative results. Our hope is the same as it has always been: that farm workers here can work together to change unjust conditions and thus to serve their brothers throughout the land."[83]

"When people are involved in something constructive, trying to bring about change, they tend to be less violent than those who are not engaged in rebuilding or in anything creative. Nonviolence forces one to be creative; it forces any leader to go to the people and get them involved so that they can come forth with new ideas. I think that once people understand the strength of nonviolence—the force it generates, the love it creates, the response that it brings from the total community—they will not be willing to abandon it easily."[84]

Notes

1. Frederick John Dalton, *The Moral Vision of César Chávez* (Maryknoll, NY: Orbis Books, 2003), p. 143.

2. Jacques Levy, *Cesar Chavez: Autobiography of La Causa* (New York: W. W. Norton & Company, 1975), p. 91.

3. Levy, *Cesar Chavez*, p. 91.

4. Levy, *Cesar Chavez*, p. 93.

5. Levy, *Cesar Chavez*, p. 184.

6. Levy, *Cesar Chavez*, p. 188.

7. Levy, *Cesar Chavez*, pp. 195–196.

8. Levy, *Cesar Chavez*, p. 267.

9. Levy, *Cesar Chavez*, p. 93.

10. Levy, *Cesar Chavez*, p. 269.

11. Levy, *Cesar Chavez*, p. 269.

12. Levy, *Cesar Chavez*, p. 269.

13. Levy, *Cesar Chavez*, p. 270.

14. Levy, *Cesar Chavez*, p. 270.

15. Levy, *Cesar Chavez*, pp. 270–271.

16. Levy, *Cesar Chavez*, p. 271.

17. Levy, *Cesar Chavez*, p. 271.

18. Levy, *Cesar Chavez*, p. 323.

19. Levy, *Cesar Chavez*, p. 323.

20. Levy, *Cesar Chavez*, p. 325.

21. Peter Matthiessen, *Sal Si Puedes: Cesar Chavez and the New American Revolution* (New York: Random House, 1969), p. 24.

22. Ronald B. Taylor, *Chavez and the Farm Workers* (Boston: Beacon Press, 1975), p. 220.

23. Taylor, *Chavez*, p. 229.

24. Taylor, *Chavez*, pp. 139–40.

25. Taylor, *Chavez*, p. 140.

26. Taylor, *Chavez*, p. 140.

27. Chávez, "Introduction," in Mark Day, *Forty Acres: Cesar Chavez and the Farm Workers* (New York: Praeger Publishers, 1971), pp. 11–12.

28. Luis Valdez and Stan Steiner, eds., *Aztlan: An Anthology of Mexican American Literature* (New York: Vintage Books, 1972), p. 387.

29. As quoted in Bob Fitch, "Tilting with the System: An Interview with Cesar Chavez," in Chris García, ed., *Chicano Politics: Readings* (New York: MSS Information Corp., 1973), n.p., originally published in *The Christian Century* (February 10, 1970), pp. 206–207.

30. John C. Hammerback and Richard J. Jensen, *The Rhetorical Career of César Chávez* (College Station: Texas A & M Press, 1998), p. 35.

31. Hammerback and Jensen, *Rhetorical Career*, p. 36.

32. Hammerback and Jensen, *Rhetorical Career*, p. 36.

33. Hammerback and Jensen, *Rhetorical Career*, p. 116.

34. Hammerback and Jensen, *Rhetorical Career*, p. 116.

35. Hammerback and Jensen, *Rhetorical Career*, p. 117.

36. Hammerback and Jensen, *Rhetorical Career*, p. 117.

37. Hammerback and Jensen, *Rhetorical Career*, p. 117.

38. Hammerback and Jensen, *Rhetorical Career*, p. 183.

39. Day, *Forty Acres*, p. 97.

40. Day, *Forty Acres*, pp. 113–114.

41. Day, *Forty Acres*, p. 114.

42. Day, *Forty Acres*, p. 114.

43. Day, *Forty Acres*, p. 191.

44. John R. Moyer, "A Conversation with César Chávez," in Matt S. Meier and Feliciano Rivera, eds., *Readings on La Raza: The Twentieth Century* (New York: Hill and Wang, 1974), pp. 253–254. First published in John R. Moyer, "A Conversation with César Chávez" in *Journal of Current Social Issues*, vol. 9, no. 3 (November–December 1970).

45. Levy, *Cesar Chavez*, p. 5.

46. Levy, *Cesar Chavez*, pp. 5–6.

47. Fitch "Tilting with the System," p. 206.

48. Susan Ferriss and Ricardo Sandoval, *The Fight in the Fields: Cesar Chavez and the Farmworkers Movement* (New York: Harcourt Brace & Company, 1997), p. 89.

49. "Tilting with the System," p. 206.

50. "Tilting with the System," p. 207.

51. "Farm Union is Alive," *Los Angeles Times*, January 2, 1975, p. 7.

52. Ferriss and Sandoval, *Fight in the Fields*, p. 97.

53. César Chávez, "Nonviolence Still Works," *Look*, April 1, 1969, p. 52.

54. "Tilting with the System," p. 207.

55. Telegram from César Chávez to Mrs. Martin Luther King, Jr., in *El Malcriado*, April 15, 1968, p. 5.

56. Richard J. Jensen and John C. Hammerback, eds., *The Words of César Chávez* (College Station: Texas A & M Press, 2002), p. 97.

57. Levy, *Cesar Chavez*, p. 227.

58. Jensen and Hammerback, *Words of César Chávez*, p. 181.

59. Jensen and Hammerback, *Words of César Chávez*, p. 96.

60. Jensen and Hammerback, *Words of César Chávez*, p. 96.

61. Dalton, *Moral Vision*, p. 99.

62. Jensen and Hammerback, *Words of César Chávez*, pp. 64–65.

63. Jensen and Hammerback, *Words of César Chávez*, p. 48.

64. Dalton, *Moral Vision*, p. 121.

65. Dalton, *Moral Vision*, pp. 127–128.

66. Dalton, *Moral Vision*, p. 138.

67. Dalton, *Moral Vision*, p. 143.

68. Jensen and Hammerback, *Words of César Chávez*, p. 25.

69. Jensen and Hammerback, *Words of César Chávez*, p. 78.

70. Jensen and Hammerback, *Words of César Chávez*, p. 96.

71. Jensen and Hammerback, *Words of César Chávez*, p. 96.

72. Jensen and Hammerback, *Words of César Chávez*, p. 167.

73. Winthrop Yinger, *Cesar Chavez: The Rhetoric of Nonviolence* (Hicksville, NY: Exposition Press, 1975), p. 75.

74. "Apostle of Non-Violence," *Observer*, May, 1970.

75. "Apostle of Non-Violence," *Observer*.

76. "Apostle of Non-Violence," *Observer*.

77. "Quotable Chavez," *Cleveland Press*, May 3, 1975.

78. "People are Willing to Sacrifice Themselves," *Fellowship*, September 1973.

79. "People are Willing."

80. "People are Willing."

81. César Chávez, "Creative Non-Violence," *The Center Magazine*, vol. 2, no. 2 (March 1969), p. 27.

82. Chávez, "Creative Non-Violence," p. 27.

83. Chávez, "Creative Non-Violence," p. 40.

84. Chávez, "Creative Non-Violence," p. 27.

CHAPTER SEVEN

~

Social Justice

As noted, César Chávez's struggle and that of the farm workers went beyond union recognition. It also involved the cause—La Causa—for social justice. César and his family had experienced racism and discrimination. But through his family socialization and self-education beginning by his reading of the papal encyclicals such as *Rerum Novarum*, he had learned about social justice. Farm workers not only needed economic improvements, but they also needed to be treated equally with other Americans. Social justice was part of César's spirituality because it was the avenue to also achieve the human dignity of the workers and of minorities such as Mexican Americans who faced injustices in work, wages, housing, education, and in other ways. To César social injustice was not only un-American, it was un-Christian. But as with other aspects of his spirituality, César's concept of social justice could not involve just wishing for it. It had to be achieved through struggle. César understood that the farm growers and their powerful allies, along with the ruling elite in the country, would not freely grant justice since they benefited, certainly economically, from injustice. Social justice had to be gained by the workers and by Mexican American themselves. It was the only way. César's spirituality involved historical agency. It involved a committed and active Christianity.

***

"Some [farm workers] had been born into the migrant stream. But we had been on the land, and I knew a different way of life. We were poor, but we had liberty. The migrant is poor, but he has no freedom."[1]

[Reflecting on the influence of his parents' involvement in farm labor organizing and participating in agricultural strikes in the 1930s and 1940s:]

"I don't want to suggest we were radical, but I know we were probably one of the strikingest families in California. We were the first ones out of the field if anybody shouted 'Huelga!' [strike!] We were constantly fighting against things that most people accepted because they didn't have the kind of beginning we had on the farm, that strong family life and family ties which we would not let anyone break. I remember times when it was a little hard to quit—we needed the money—but we didn't consider that. Out attitude was, we have to do it, and we accepted it."[2]

"While we do not belittle or underestimate our adversaries, for they are the rich and powerful and possess the land, we are not afraid nor do we cringe from the confrontation. We welcome it! We have planned for it. We know our cause is just, that history is a story of social revolution and that the poor should inherit the land."[3]

"It is not good enough to know why we are oppressed and by whom. We must join the struggle for what is right and just! Jesus does not promise it will be an easy way to live life and his own life certainly points in a hard direction; but he does promise we will be 'satisfied' (not stuffed, but satisfied). He promises that by giving life we will find life—full, meaningful life as God meant it to be."[4]

"Our opponents in the agricultural industry are very powerful, and farm workers are still weak in money and influence. But we have another kind of power that comes from the justice of our cause. So long as we are willing to sacrifice for that cause, so long as we persist in nonviolence and work to spread the message of our struggle, then millions of people around the world will respond from their hearts, will support our efforts, and in the end we will overcome. It can be done. We know it can be done. God give us the strength and patience to do it without bitterness so that we can win both our friends and opponents to the cause of justice."[5]

"We are suffering. We have suffered, and we are not afraid to suffer in order to win our cause. We have suffered unnumbered ills and crimes in the name of the law of the land. Our men, women, and children have suffered not only the basic brutality of stoop labor, and the most obvious injustices of the system; they have also suffered the desperation of knowing that that system caters to the greed of callous men and not to our needs. Now we will suffer for the purpose of ending the poverty, the misery, and the injustice, with the hope that our children will not be exploited as we have been. They have imposed hunger on us, and now we hunger for justice. We draw our strength from the very despair in which we have been forced to live. WE SHALL ENDURE."[6]

"We made a solemn promise: to enjoy our rightful part of the riches of this land, to throw off the yoke of being considered as agricultural employees or slaves. We are free men and we demand justice."[7]

"Rebel against the injustice of your grower. Revolt against the injustice of your labor contractor. God is witness that what you ask for is just. God is witness to the abuses that have been committed against you. God is witness and judge and will judge in the near feature. All the abuses are against the dignity of man, who is made by God in his own image."[8]

"The solution to this deadly crisis will not be found in the arrogance of the powerful but in solidarity with the weak and the helpless. I pray to God that this fast [1988] will be a preparation for a multitude of simple deeds for justice, carried out by men and women whose hearts are focused on the suffering of the poor and who yearn, with us, for a better world. Together, all things are possible."[9]

"If I'm going to save my soul, it's going to be through the struggle for justice."[10]

"We want radical change. Nothing short of radical change is going to have any impact on our lives or our problems. We want sufficient power to control our destinies. This is our struggle. It's a lifetime job. The work for social change and against social injustice is never ended."[11]

"We seek our basic God-given rights as human beings. Because we have suffered and are not afraid to suffer—in order to survive we are ready to give up everything, even our lives, in our fight for social justice. We shall do it without violence because that is our destiny."[12]

"Truth is justice. If you stick to truth, it seems to me, you can overturn mountains."[13]

"We are a family bound together in a common struggle for justice. We are a Union family celebrating our unity and the nonviolent nature of our movement."[14]

"The ranchers should know . . . that all our sacrifices, our sweat, tears, and blood have a focus, a very important ideal. This ideal is an impulse toward sacrifice, it is the ideal of justice."[15]

"A new order of things is replacing the old in agriculture. It can be replaced peacefully with the consent of the employers, or it can proceed by painful struggle. We are entering a just and necessary struggle, not of our choosing, but a struggle we have been forced into. Everything we have done, we have done in good faith. Our good faith has been received with a slap in the face of the farm workers."[16]

"I contend that not only the American public but people in general throughout the world will respond to a cause that involves injustice. It's just natural to want to be with the underdog. In a boxing match, however popular the champion may be, if he begins to really get the other guy and beat him up bad, there is a natural tendency to go with the underdog. And in the struggle it's not a contest between two people or a team but a contest between a lot of people who are poor and others who are wealthy."[17]

"'Hay más tiempo que vida'—that's one of our *dichos* [proverbs]. 'There is more time than life.' We don't worry about time, because time and history are on our side."[18]

"We feel that freedom is lost when it is not defended. And we intend to defend our freedom. We feel that a jail with bars is no worse than a jail without bars."[19]

"[J]ail is a small price to pay to keep fighting injustice."[20]

[César was jailed in Salinas on December 4, 1970, when he refused a judge's order to call off the boycott of lettuce. He was released on December 24, 1970, and stated:]
   "Jails were made for men who fight for their rights. My spirit was never in jail. They can jail us, but they can never jail the Cause."[21]

"No, I am not a communist. But I am not saying this because people are accusing me of being one. I'm saying this because I'm a Christian, and I am proud of that."[22]

"[T]rue justice for ourselves and our opponents is only possible before God, who is the final judge."[23]

"Men who are seeking justice are not going to be stopped by unjust decisions."[24]

"The work for social change and against social injustice is never ended."[25]

[In 1972, César opposed antilabor union legislation in Arizona aimed at preventing the organizing of farm workers. As part of his opposition, he engaged in a twenty-four-day fast:]

   "My concern is the spirit of fear that lies behind such laws in the hearts of growers and legislators across the country. Somehow these powerful men and women must be helped to realize that there is nothing to fear from treating their workers as fellow human beings."[26]

"It's unfortunate that power is needed to get justice. That suggests a lot about the nature of man. And we also must guard against too much power, because power corrupts, but that was not one of our problems then."[27]

"The time has come when powerless and small groups of people, minority people . . . cannot be set aside or pushed aside without explanation."[28]

"[T]here are many changes in the church today. But many of these changes, like the new ritual of the mass, are merely external. What I like to see is a priest get up and speak about things like racism and poverty. But, even when you hear about these things from the pulpit, you get the feeling that they aren't doing anything significant to alleviate these evils. They are just talking about them."[29]

"You know . . . the church could really help the Chicanos right now. It could change the social order for the better. It could really be in the forefront of a revolution for human dignity. I don't want to see the people walk away from it. But it's happening, you know."[30]

"If our work is considered Communistic by some, there's nothing we can do about it, but I'm not willing to admit that we Christians are not more willing to fight for social justice."[31]

"[I]n a nutshell, what do we want the Church to do? We don't ask for more cathedrals. We don't ask for bigger churches or fine gifts. We ask for its presence with us, besides us, as Christ among us. We ask the Church to *sacrifice with the people* for social change, for justice, and for love of brother. We don't ask for words. We ask for deeds. We don't ask for paternalism. We ask for servant hood."[32]

"It is always a mistake to get involved in proving that the other person is wrong and defending your own good name. You lose in the long run because you let the main issue get mixed up with these other things."[33]

"We are men locked in a death struggle against man's inhumanity to man."[34]

"For me, Christianity happens to be a natural source of faith. I have read what Christ said when he was here. He was very clear in what he meant and knew exactly what he was after. He was extremely radical and he was for social change."[35]

"The only justice is Christ—God's justice. We're the victims of a lot of shenanigans by the courts but ultimately, down the line, real justice comes. It . . . comes from God's hand."[36]

"In the beginning, the UFW attacked the source of shame with which our people lived. We attacked injustice and poor living conditions, not by complaining, not by seeking hand-outs, not by becoming soldiers in the War on Poverty, but by organizing."[37]

"We want radical change. Nothing short of radical change is going to have any impact on our lives or our problems. We want sufficient power to control our destinies. This is our struggle. It's a lifetime job. The work for social change and against social injustice is never ended."[38]

"I learned what life teaches all generations, that one must fight for justice and truth. You can't sit around and complain. You've got to get down to it and make demands."[39]

"I was convinced [that my ideology was] very Christian. That's my interpretation. I don't think it was so much political or economic."[40]

"Fighting for social justice is one of the most profound ways in which man can say yes to man's dignity, and that really means sacrifice."[41]

"Regardless of what the future holds for our union, regardless of what the future holds for farm workers, our accomplishments cannot be undone. The consciousness and the pride that were raised by our union are alive and thriving inside millions of young Hispanics who will never work on a farm."[42]

"I've always maintained that it isn't the form that's going to make the difference. It isn't the rule or the procedure or the ideology, but it's human beings that will make it. Society is made up of groups, and so long as the smaller groups do not have the same rights and the same protection as others—I don't care whether you call it capitalism or Communism—it is not going to work. Somehow, the guys in power have to be reached by counterpower, or through a change in their hearts and minds, or change will not come."[43]

Notes

1. Susan Ferriss and Ricardo Sandoval, *The Fight in the Fields: Cesar Chavez and the Farmworkers Movement* (New York: Harcourt Brace & Company, 1997), p. 18.

2. David Goodwin, *Cesar Chavez: Hope for the People* (New York: Fawcett Columbine, 1991), p. 111.

3. John C. Hammerback and Richard J. Jensen, *The Rhetorical Career of César Chávez* (College Station: Texas A & M Press, 1998), p. 3.

4. *National Catholic Reporter*, March 7, 1975.

5. Richard J. Jensen and John C. Hammerback, eds., *The Words of César Chávez* (College Station: Texas A & M Press, 2002), p. 168.

6. Jensen and Hammerback, *Words of César Chávez*, p. 17.

7. Winthrop Yinger, *Cesar Chavez: The Rhetoric of Nonviolence* (Hicksville, NY: Exposition Press, 1975), p. 63.

8. Frederick John Dalton, *The Moral Vision of César Chávez* (Maryknoll, NY: Orbis Books, 2003), p. 98.

9. Dalton, *Moral Vision*, p. 136.

10. Dalton, *Moral Vision*, p. 137.

11. Dalton, *Moral Vision*, p. 81.

12. Gilberto López y Rivas, ed., *The Chicano: Life and Struggles of the Mexican Movement in the United States* (New York: Monthly Review Press, 1973), p. 108.

13. Ronald B. Taylor, *Chavez and the Farm Workers* (Boston: Beacon Press, 1975), p. 139.

14. Hammerback and Jensen, *Rhetorical Career*, p. 90.

15. Hammerback and Jensen, *Rhetorical Career*, p. 168.

16. Jane Marie Yett, "Farm Labor Struggles in California, 1970–1973, in Light of Reinhold Niebuhr's Concepts of Power and Justice," unpublished Ph.D. dissertation, Graduate Theological Union, Berkeley, 1980, p. 132.

17. Bob Fitch "Tilting with the System," *The Christian Century* (Feb. 10, 1970), p. 204.

18. Peter Matthiessen, *Sal Si Puedes: Cesar Chavez and the New American Revolution* (New York: Random House, 1969), p. 35.

19. Jacques Levy, *Cesar Chavez: Autobiography of La Causa* (New York: W. W. Norton & Company, 1975), p. 417.

20. Taylor, *Chavez*, p. 261.

21. Levy, *Cesar Chavez*, p. 433.

22. Mark Day, *Forty Acres: Cesar Chavez and the Farm Workers* (New York: Praeger Publishers, 1971), p. 67.

23. Hammerback and Jensen, *Rhetorical Career*, p. 152.

24. Levy, *Cesar Chavez*, p. 389.

25. Levy, *Cesar Chavez*, p. 538.

26. Levy, *Cesar Chavez*, p. 463.

27. Levy, *Cesar Chavez*, p. 110.

28. John C. Hammerback, Richard J. Jensen, and José Angel Gutiérrez, *A War of Words: Chicano Protest in the 1960s and 1970s* (Westport, CT: Greenwood Press, 1985), p. 44.

29. Day, *Forty Acres*, p. 58.

30. Day, *Forty Acres*, p. 59.

31. Matthiesen, *Sal Si Puedes*, p. 268.

32. Chávez, "The Mexican-American and the Church," in F. Chris García, ed., *La Causa Politica: A Chicano Political Reader* (Notre Dame: University of Notre Dame Press, 1974), p. 146.

33. "Quotable Chavez," *Cleveland Press*, May 3, 1975.

34. Hammerback and Jensen, *Rhetorical Career*, p. 30.

35. Levy, *Cesar Chavez*, p. 27.

36. Dalton, *Moral Vision*, p. 80.

37. Dalton, *Moral Vision*, p. 80.

38. Dalton, *Moral Vision*, p. 81.

39. "Cesar Chavez Looks Back on Long Struggle," *Imperial Valley News*, April 25, 1972, in Anne Loftis Collection, Box 8, Fld. 2 in Special Collections, Green Library, Stanford University.

40. Richard Griswold del Castillo and Richard A. García, *César Chávez: A Triumph of Spirit* (Norman: University of Oklahoma Press, 1995), p. 111.

41. Goodwin, *Cesar Chavez*, p. 231.

42. Ferriss and Sandoval, *Fight in the Fields*, p. 248.

43. John R. Moyer, "A Conversation with César Chávez," in Matt S. Meier and Feliciano Rivera, *Readings on La Raza: The Twentieth Century* (New York: Hill and Wang, 1974), p. 253.

Farm workers on pilgrimage to Sacramento, spring 1966. Copyright ©1966 George Ballis/Take Stock.

CHAPTER EIGHT

~

Pilgrimage

Seeing the farm workers' struggle as part of a larger spiritual one for the human and sacred dignity of the workers, César Chávez integrated his union's demonstrations with religious and spiritual connotations. After several months of the grape strike with no success in pressuring the growers to negotiate with the union, César decided to emulate the black civil rights movement by organizing a twenty-five-day protest march from Delano to Sacramento in the spring of 1966. But as with almost everything he did, the march also became a spiritual exercise. Calling the march a *peregrinación* or pilgrimage, César stressed that the participants—including himself—besides bringing attention to the strike would also take the opportunity to do penance not only for their individual sins, but as a way of preparing themselves for the long hard struggle against the growers. Based on the Mexican religious tradition of pilgrimage, César knew that this concept would be familiar to his largely Mexican American supporters. To add to the spiritual nature of the *peregrinación*, the marchers carried the image of Our Lady of Guadalupe along with the cross. Finally, the pilgrimage concluded on Easter Sunday. After their sacrifice, resurrection awaited the participants. Other marches would convey similar religious and spiritual symbolism.

***

[Working with the Community Service Organization (CSO) from 1958 through 1959 in Oxnard combating the Bracero Program and its discrimination against Mexican American workers, César staged a march through Oxnard with 10,000 supporters in April 1959:]

"That's when I discovered the power of the march. We started with a couple of hundred people into La Colonia [the Mexican barrio] and by the time we got through, we must have had ten thousand people. Everybody was in it. Among Mexicans a march has a very special attraction. It appeals to them—just like a pilgrimage."[1]

"[I]n January [1965], a priest came to Delano and talked of the coming Lenten season. It reminded some of the strikers from Mexico of the Lenten pilgrimage they had made."[2]

"In every religious oriented culture 'the pilgrimage' has had a place, a trip made with sacrifice and hardship as an expression of penance and of commitment—and often involving a petition to the patron of the pilgrimage for some sincerely sought benefit of body or soul. Pilgrimage has not passed from Mexican culture. Daily at any of the major shrines of the country, and in particular at the Basilica of the Lady of Guadalupe, there arrive pilgrims from all points—some of whom may have long since walked-out the pieces of rubber tire that once served them as soles, and many of whom will walk on their knees the last mile or so of the pilgrimage. Many of the 'pilgrims' of Delano will have walked such pilgrimages themselves in their lives—perhaps as very small children even; and cling to the memory of the day-long, marches, the camps at night, streams forded, hills climbed, the sacral aura of the sanctuary and the 'fiesta' that followed. But throughout the Spanish speaking world there is another tradition that touches the present march, that of the Lenten penitential processions, where the *penitentes* would march through the streets, often in sack cloth and ashes, some even carrying crosses as a sign of penance for their sins, and as a plea for the mercy of God. The penitential procession is also in the blood of the Mexican American, and the Delano march [1966] will therefore be one of penance—public penance for the sins of the strikers, their own personal sins as well as their yielding perhaps to feelings of hatred and revenge in the strike itself. They hope by the march to set themselves at peace with the Lord, so that the justice of their cause will be purified of all lesser motivation. . . . Pilgrimage, penance and revolution. The pilgrimage from Delano to Sacramento has strong religio-cultural overtones. But it is also the pilgrimage of a cultural minority who have suffered from a hostile environment, and a minority who means business."[3]

"We are conscious of the historical significance of our Pilgrimage. It is clearly evident that our path travels through a valley well known to all Mexican farm workers. We know all of these towns of Delano, Madera, Fresno, Modesto, Stockton and Sacramento, because along this very same road, in this very same valley, the Mexican race has sacrificed itself for the last hundred years. Our sweat and our blood have fallen on this land to make other men rich. This Pilgrimage is a witness to the suffering we have seen for generations."[4]

"The Penance we accept symbolizes the suffering we shall have in order to bring justice to these same towns, to this same valley. The Pilgrimage we make symbolizing the long historical road we have traveled in this valley alone, and the long road we have yet to travel, with much penance, in order to bring about the Revolution we need."[5]

"We seek, and have, the support of the Church in what we do. At the head of the Pilgrimage we carry LA VIRGEN DE LA GUADALUPE (the Virgin of Guadalupe) because she is ours, all ours, Patroness of the Mexican people. We also carry the Sacred Cross and the Star of David because we are not sectarians, and because we ask the help and prayers of all religions."[6]

"[T]he centuries-old religious tradition of Spanish culture conjoins with the very contemporary cultural syndrome of 'demonstration' springing from the spontaneity of the poor, the downtrodden, the rejected, the discriminated against bearing visibly their need and demand for equality and freedom."[7]

"We timed the twenty-five-day march so we'd arrive in Sacramento on Easter Sunday."[8]

"Equally important to me—and I don't know how many share my thoughts on this—was that this was an excellent way of training ourselves to endure the long, long struggle, which by this time had become evident. So this was a penance more than anything else—and it was quite a penance, because there was an awful lot of suffering involved in this pilgrimage, a great deal of pain."[9]

"We wanted to be fit not only physically but also spiritually, and we wanted to stress nonviolence even more, build confidence, and have more visible nonviolent tactics."[10]

"At the front we had the American flag, the Mexican flag, the flag from the Philippines, and the banner of Our Lady of Guadalupe."[11]

"This pilgrimage [1966] is a witness to the suffering we have seen for generations. The penance we accept symbolizes the suffering we shall have in order to bring justice to these same towns, to this same valley. This is the beginning of a social movement in fact and not in pronouncements."[12]

[These quotes are from the article "Farm Workers Pilgrimage" in *El Malcriado* (March 17, 1966), pp. 4–5, and are related to the march from Delano to Sacramento in 1966. Although not written by César, they are reflective of his views and authorized by him:]

"Fifty farm workers set out this week to march 300 miles, in the greatest pilgrimage in California's history. They will march from Delano to the Cathedral in Sacramento, and will pass through hundreds of little valley towns and communities on the way. This Lenten Pilgrimage will be led by Our Lady of Guadalupe, whose statue will be carried the whole way on the shoulders of farm workers. It will arrive in Sacramento for Easter, which for Christians everywhere symbolizes the Day of Liberation for all mankind. For Christ suffered, died, and rose again, that we all might be free. The pilgrimage will be dedicated to our faith in God, in the God of justice, who brought His people out of slavery in Egypt;

Who freed His people from the Babylonians; Who conquered the mighty Roman Empire, not with the sword, but with love. The pilgrimage will also be dedicated to those great movements of men which have tried to improve the world and bring to God's children the justice that He promised them. The pilgrimage will signify our commitment to this cause of Justice. . . . Farm workers *are* revolutionaries, as are all true Christians, because they are trying to change the world, to end the evil, the injustice, the bitterness that lie at the root of so much of the sins of this world. . . . The march is not a 'protest march,' but a pilgrimage in affirmation of our faith in God and our faith in the promises of our forefathers, and our commitment to our cause. But while this will be a march of faith, a march signifying the strikers' commitment to the cause, it will also be a march of penance. For Lent is the time when Christians ask for forgiveness of their sins, where they act through public penance to purify themselves of their sins."[13]

"When the pilgrims arrive in a town, they will have a meeting and tell the people about the pilgrimage and its causes. They will tell the people about the faith that sustains the pilgrimage, and the faith that sustains the strike in the grapes, and the struggle of farm workers for justice."[14]

"Finally after four weeks of walking, the pilgrims will reach Sacramento. On that last day, everyone will be invited to join the pilgrims, in a triumphant procession in the City and to the Church, for a solemn High Mass. . . . In the Church, the pilgrims will thank the Lord for the aid and many blessings He has given to farm workers in the last six months in their struggles for justice. And they will pray for forgiveness for those transgressions for which they have been guilty."[15]

[From the Plan de Delano (1966):]

"We the undersigned, gathered in Pilgrimage to every agricultural area of the United States, make penance for all the needs of Farm Workers. As free and sovereign men and women, we do solemnly declare before the civilized world which judges our actions, and before the nation where we work, the proposition we have formulated to end the injustice that oppresses us."[16]

Notes

1. Jacques Levy, *Cesar Chavez: Autobiography of La Causa* (New York: W. W. Norton & Company, 1975), p. 141.

2. Levy, *Cesar Chavez*, p. 206.

3. Richard J. Jensen and John C. Hammerback, eds., *The Words of César Chávez* (College Station: Texas A & M Press, 2002), pp. 15–16.

4. Jensen and Hammerback, *Words of César Chávez*, p. 16.

5. Jensen and Hammerback, *Words of César Chávez*, p. 16.

6. Jensen and Hammerback, *Words of César Chávez*, p. 17.

7. John C. Hammerback and Richard J. Jensen, *The Rhetorical Career of César Chávez* (College Station: Texas A & M Press, 1998), p. 40.

8. Levy, *Cesar Chavez*, p. 207.

9. Levy, *Cesar Chavez*, p. 207.

10. Levy, *Cesar Chavez*, p. 207.

11. Levy, *Cesar Chavez*, p. 208.

12. "Plan de Delano," in Gilberto López y Rivas, ed., *The Chicanos: Life and Struggles of the Mexican Minority in the United States* (New York: Monthly Review Press, 1973), p. 108.

13. "Farm Workers Pilgrimage," *El Malcriado*, March 17, 1966, p. 4.

14. "Farm Workers Pilgrimage," p. 5.

15. "Farm Workers Pilgrimage," p. 5.

16. Hammerback and Jensen, *Rhetorical Career*, p. 93.

César Chávez breaking twenty-five-day fast by taking Holy Communion with Senator Robert Kennedy (center) and Helen Chávez (far left) in Delano, California, March 10, 1968. UCLA Department of Special Collections, Charles E. Young Research Library.

CHAPTER NINE

~

Fasting

A very important aspect of César Chávez's spirituality involved fasting. Fasting, as César often observed, was not the same as a hunger strike that was aimed at achieving a political goal. Fasting, for him, was personal, collective, and, above all, spiritual. While clearly influenced by the example of Gandhi's fasts, César also resorted to the Mexican Catholic tradition of doing penance. Beginning with his famous 1968 twenty-five-day fast, the first of many, César fasted for his own sins and for those of his supporters. On this particular occasion, he especially wanted to do so in order to reinforce the principle of nonviolence. Other fasts brought attention to the suffering of the farm workers and the need for social justice. Fasting and its spiritual connotations, according to César, was also a very effective way of communicating a message to others. In the following quotes, he describes both the physical and emotional reactions to this form of penance. Many believe that César's many fasts, although effective, at the same time physically weakened him and contributed to his death in 1993.

***

"I pray to God that this fast will be a preparation for a multiple of simple deeds for justice, carried out by men and women whose hearts are focused on the suffering of the poor and who yearn, with us, for a better world."[1]

"As I look back at this past year [1988], I can see many events that precipitated the fast, including the terrible suffering of farm workers and their children, the crushing of farm workers' rights, the denial of fair and free elections and the death of good faith collective bargaining in California agriculture. All of these events are connected with the great cause of justice for farm worker families."[2]

"Fasting is probably the most powerful communicative tool that we have. . . . It communicates, but not through the written or expressed way. Fasting communicates through the soul. . . . [I]t is the most potent way to communicate that I've ever seen."[3]

[Ending a twenty-four-day "fast for justice" in Phoenix, June 4, 1972:]
    "I am weak in my body but I feel very strong in my spirit. I am happy to end the Fast because it is not an easy thing. But it is also not easy for my family and for many of you who have worried and worked and sacrificed. The Fast was meant as a call to sacrifice for justice and a reminder of how much suffering there is among farm workers. In fact, what is a few days without food in comparison to the daily pain of our brothers and sisters who do backbreaking work in the fields under inhumane conditions and without hope of ever breaking their cycle of poverty and misery. What a terrible irony it is that the very people who harvest the food we eat do not have enough food for their own children."[4]

"The fast is a very personal spiritual thing, and it's not done out of recklessness. It's not done out of a desire to destroy myself, but it's done out of a deep conviction that we can communicate to people, either those who are for us or against us, faster and more effectively *spiritually* than we can in any other way."[5]

"The fast [1988] was first and foremost a personal act. It was something I felt compelled to do—to purify my own body, mind, and soul."[6]

"The fast [1988] was also an act of penance for those in positions of moral authority and for all men and women who know what is right and just. It is for those who know that they could or should do more. It is for those who, by their failure to act, become bystanders in the poisoning of our food and the people who produce it."[7]

"[The fast, 1988] is directed at myself. Do we carry in our hearts the suffering of farm workers and their children? Do we feel their pain deeply enough? I know I don't—and I am ashamed."[8]

[After the twenty-five-day fast in 1968:]
    "I undertook this fast [1968] because my heart was filled with grief and pain for the suffering of farm workers. The fast was first for me and then for all of us in this union. It was a fast for nonviolence and a call to sacrifice."[9]

[At the conclusion of the twenty-five-day fast, February 15–March 10, 1968, in Delano:]
    "We are gathered here today not so much to observe the end of the Fast but because we are a family bound together in a common struggle for justice. We are a Union family celebrating our unity and the nonviolent nature of our movement. Perhaps in the future we will come together at other times and places to break bread and to renew our courage and to celebrate important victories."[10]

[On the 1967 strike against Perelli-Minetti Brothers winery and negotiations in Burlingame:]
    "When we left Burlingame that Friday, everything was ready to be signed on Tuesday. My prayers were answered, I thought, how can I give thanks? I decided fasting would be a good way, from Friday to Tuesday when the contract would be signed. What started as a thanksgiving fast—giving thanks for saving the Union—changed when the signing was delayed. 'I can't eat until he signs,' I thought. At that point, although Perelli-Minetti didn't know about it, the fast became more like a hunger strike. I didn't tell anyone I was fasting. I continued working. Day followed day, as the next weekend came around, but they still

hadn't signed. I was sick, both mentally and physically, as I hadn't prepared myself mentally for a fast. Before they signed on the thirteenth
day, I thought I would die. But after a couple of days in bed, I was
okay."[11]

"I couldn't really understand Gandhi until I was actually in the fast
[1968]; then the book became much more clear. Things I understood
but didn't feel—well, in the fast I *felt* them, and there were some real
insights. There wasn't a day or a night that I lost. I slept in the day
when I could, and at night, and I read. I slept on a very thin mattress.
. . . And I had the peace of mind that is so important; the fasting part
is secondary."[12]

[During his 1968 fast, Chavez was asked if he had any hallucinations:]
   "I was wide awake. But there are certain things that happened, about
the third or fourth day—and this has happened to me every time I've
fasted—it's like all of a sudden when you're up at a high altitude, and
you clear your ears; in the same way, my mind clears, it is open to everything. After a long conversation, for example, I could repeat word for
word what had been said. That's one of the sensations of the fast, it's
beautiful. And usually I can't concentrate on music well, but in the fast,
I could see the whole orchestra and everything, that music was so
clear."[13]

"After the twenty-first day of the [1968] fast, Helen, Richard [his
brother], his wife Sally, and one or two of the kids were with me. They
were very worried about my health. While we were talking, all of a sudden I said, 'Oh, do you hear the music?'"
   "'We don't hear anything.'
   "'Yea, there's music.'
   "When I said it the third time, 'Yea, that's really nice music. Where's
it coming from?' they all looked at me and at each other as if I were
crazy.
   "I demanded that they investigate."
   "Richard went out and just looked around a little bit. 'No, there's
nobody playing.'
   "'Richard, somebody is singing Mexican songs, and they are playing.'

"'Oh, you're crazy.'

"'I know there's somebody doing it.' Then I began to wonder, am I really going crazy? So I said, 'You have to go out there and look.'

"He went way over by the dump at the other end of Forty Acres [the farm workers' compound] and there were a group of guys there drinking and singing."

"And I could hear it that far away, while in the room behind the closed metal door and in spite of adobe wall eight to ten inches thick."[14]

"The solution to this deadly crisis will not be found in the arrogance of the powerful but in solidarity with the weak and the helpless. I pray to God that this [1988] fast will be a preparation for a multitude of simple deeds for justice, carried out by men and women whose hearts are focused on the suffering of the poor and who yearn, with us, for a better world. Together, all things are possible."[15]

[César did his first major fast starting on February 15, 1968, due to threats of violence by some of his followers:]

"Then I talked about violence. How could they oppose the violence of the war in Vietnam, I asked, but propose that we use violence for our Cause? When the Civil Rights Movement turned to violence, I said, it was the blacks who suffered, who were killed, who had their homes burned. If we turned to violence, it would be the poor who would suffer."[16]

"Once we started with the religious service [daily mass at the Forty Acres compound], the fast affected our members in a very religious way, supporting me. They brought many offerings, the largest number being crucifixes and Christ in many forms. Many others brought the Virgin of Guadalupe, while the third most popular gift was St. Martín de Porres, the black saint from Peru, who is the most popular saint in Latin America."[17]

"There was a lot of personal communication in the fast. The people came and I would say one word or two, and they understood. To some it was very emotional. They were very worried about my dying."[18]

"While the fast had tremendous effect and developed strength in many ways, very few people supported me—wanted me to keep fasting. Most people were worried, though for different reasons. . . . Very few people could see all the spiritual and psychological and political good that was coming out of it, good which I had no idea was going to happen."[19]

"I have just begun the seventh day of a personal fast of penance and hope. After so many months of struggle and slow progress, I have become fearful that our common commitment to nonviolence is weakening and that we may take dangerous shortcuts to victory. I accept full responsibility for this temptation and for all of its possible negative results. Our hope is the same as it has always been: that the farm workers here can work together to change unjust conditions and thus to serve their brothers throughout the land."[20]

"After about seven days, I got away from all the physical pain. I did not want food. I saw it and rejected it. And I was surprised how little sleep I needed, only two or three hours of it at one time. I spent more time awake than sleeping."[21]

"It wasn't until later that the other pains came, the leg pains and back pains. I think that because of a lack of calcium, I began to draw calcium from my bones. The pains in my joints were horrible. But that was later, after more than two weeks of not eating."[22]

"After seven days it was like going into a different dimension. I began to see things in a different perspective, to retain a lot more, to develop tremendous power of concentration."[23]

"I had a lot of time to examine my past, and I was able to develop self-criticism and examination. I began to see that there were more important things than some of the problems that upset me, such as my administrative problems. I lost most of my emotional attachments to them."[24]

"It wasn't that saving my soul was more important than the strike. On the contrary, I said to myself, if I'm going to save my soul, it's going to be through the struggle for social justice."[25]

[During the lettuce strike in the Salinas Valley in 1970, a local judge issued a restraining order to stop the picketing. César refused to obey it,
believing it was unconstitutional, and started a fast to protest the order:]

"That fast was not like a spiritual fast. It was mostly because I was
distressed, and I needed strength. Because the Teamsters had broken
their agreement, there was a lot of hatred building up. It wasn't clear in
my mind what I would do in case violence broke out on our side. I also
wanted to try and get the proper perspective of what was happening in
Salinas."[26]

[During César's July 1984 fast:]

"[While the fast] is first and foremost personal, directed at myself . . .
for the purification of my own body, mind, and soul, the fast is also a
heart felt prayer for purification and strengthening for all of us—for myself and for all those who work beside me in the farm workers movement, whatever the work we do."[27]

[Dolores Huerta on César's 1968 fast:]

"Poor Cesar! They just couldn't accept it for what it was. I know it's
hard for people who are not Mexican to understand, but this is part of
the Mexican culture—the penance, the whole idea of suffering for
something, of self-inflicted punishment. It's a tradition of very long
standing. In fact, Cesar has often mentioned in speeches that we will
not win through violence, we will win through fasting and prayer."[28]

"Sometimes you must withstand pressures from your friends and your family as well as from your enemies. And when it comes to fasting, I don't negotiate. Once I'm on a fast, I'm on a different level. Patience is infinite. I
could say no and no and no a thousand times and not get sick about saying no. Some people have died from fasting in fifteen days, some in
twenty, but I don't know if they died because they were unable to assess
the situation. Yet you're not afraid of that, either. Maybe what happens is
you go on a fast, and get feeling so great you're not even afraid of death."[29]

"My first public fast for the cause was in Delano in 1968, when I fasted
for 25 days. I fasted for 24 days in 1972, in Arizona. There have been

other, shorter fasts also. But they were not intended as a pressure against the growers. They were first for me and then for all of us in the movement. Some people don't understand the difference between a fast and a hunger strike. A hunger strike is an act of protest directed against an opponent. A fast is first an internal spiritual act and is not intended as a weapon against anyone. The 1968 fast was designed to call the union back to the nonviolent roots upon which it was founded. The Arizona fast was meant as a call to sacrifice and a reminder of how much suffering there is among farm workers. Both fasts were successful. After the Delano fast the farm workers persisted in their struggle with the grape growers without violence and won a momentous victory when the growers signed contracts in 1970. After the 1972 Phoenix fast, the farm workers joined with other progressive elements in Arizona in turning around the political and social order there. I was happy to end both fasts because they were not easy things, especially for my family. After the first fast, it took me a long time to fully recover. I fast regularly now. But they are private affairs and since then I have learned a great deal about fasting so it is not as much of a physical strain."[30]

[Regarding the fast of 1968:]

". . . to bring the Movement to a halt, to do something that would force them and me to deal with the whole questions of violence and ourselves. I told them I thought they were discouraged, because they were talking about short cuts, about violence. They were getting so mad with the growers, that they couldn't be effective anymore. . . . Then I said I was going to stop eating until such time as everyone in the strike either ignored me or made up their minds that they were not going to be committing violence."[31]

"My fast is informed by my religious faith and by my deep roots in the Church. It is not intended as pressure on anyone but only is an expression of my own deep feelings and my own need to do penance and to be in prayer."[32]

"Nonviolence can only be used by those whose cause is strong. It is very hard and man's self-control is very weak. I am not completely nonviolent yet, and I know it. That's is why I fasted; I felt it was a very personal form of self-testing and of prayer."[33]

Notes

1. Frederick John Dalton, *The Moral Vision of César Chávez* (Maryknoll, NY: Orbis Books, 2003), pp. 18–19.

2. Dalton, *Moral Vision*, p. 135.

3. Dalton, *Moral Vision*, p. 137.

4. Richard J. Jensen and John C. Hammerback, eds., *The Words of César Chávez* (College Station: Texas A & M Press, 2002), p. 167.

5. Jacques Levy, *Cesar Chavez: Autobiography of La Causa* (New York: W. W. Norton & Company, 1975), p. 465.

6. Jensen and Hammerback, *Words of César Chávez*, p. 169.

7. Jensen and Hammerback, *Words of César Chávez*, p. 169.

8. "Fast by Chavez Over Pesticides Passes Twenty-Ninth Day," *The New York Times*, August 16, 1988, p. A18.

9. John C. Hammerback and Richard J. Jensen, *The Rhetorical Career of César Chávez* (College Station: Texas A & M Press, 1998), p. 91.

10. "Statement by César Chávez read by Rev. James Drake to nearly 8,000 farm workers, March 10, 1968 at the conclusion of a 25 day Fast for Non-Violence," as printed in Berthat Rhodes Backus, "A Communicator for 'La Causa': A Burkeian Analysis of the Rhetoric of César Chávez," Ph.D. dissertation, University of California, Santa Barbara, 1970, p. 99.

11. Levy, *Cesar Chavez*, p. 261.

12. Peter Matthiessen, *Sal Si Puedes: Cesar Chavez and the New American Revolution* (New York: Random House, 1969), p. 187.

13. Matthiessen, *Sal Si Puedes*, p. 187.

14. Levy, *Cesar Chavez*, p. 284.

15. Dalton, *Moral Vision*, p. 136.

16. Levy, *Cesar Chavez*, p. 273.

17. Levy, *Cesar Chavez*, p. 275.

18. Levy, *Cesar Chavez*, p. 275.

19. Levy, *Cesar Chavez*, pp. 275–276.

20. Winthrop Yinger, *Cesar Chavez: The Rhetoric of Nonviolence* (Hicksville, NY: Exposition Press, 1975), p. 40.

21. Levy, *Cesar Chavez*, p. 276.

22. Levy, *Cesar Chavez*, p. 276.

23. Levy, *Cesar Chavez*, p. 276.

24. Levy, *Cesar Chavez*, p. 276.
25. Levy, *Cesar Chavez*, p. 276.
26. Levy, *Cesar Chavez*, p. 340.
27. Hammerback and Jensen, *Rhetorical Career*, p. 186.
28. Levy, *Cesar Chavez*, p. 277.
29. Levy, *Cesar Chavez*, p. 350.
30. "We Are Still Fighting For Our Lives," *Visitor*, November 11, 1980.
31. Pat Hoffman, *Ministry of the Dispossessed: Learning from the Farm Worker Movement* (Los Angeles: Wallace Press, 1987), p. 41.
32. Yinger, *Cesar Chavez*, p. 65.
33. Dalton, *Moral Vision*, p. 143.

CHAPTER TEN

~

On Gandhi

There is no question but that one of the major influences on César Chávez was Mahatma Gandhi, the great spiritual and political leader of India's independence from the British Empire. Father Donald McDonnell in San Jose introduced César to the life and spiritual practices of Gandhi in the late 1940s. It's not clear how much of Gandhi's own writings César read, but he did first read Louis Fischer's biography of Gandhi. It was from Gandhi that the farm worker leader noted the power of nonviolence and of the importance of spiritual leadership that would also characterize César's work.

***

"I understand Gandhi more and more. To him duty was the first call. . . . I want to experiment with some of the things he did but not imitate him, because I don't think that can be done. He had tremendous discipline, both personal and around him."[1]

"Then of course, there were the more personal things, the whole question of the spirit versus the body. He prepared himself for it by his diet, starving his body so that his spirit could overtake it, controlling the palate, then controlling the sex urge, then using all of his energies to do nothing but service. He was very tough with himself."[2]

"Not too long ago I was speaking to a group of Indians including three who had worked with Gandhi. When I said I thought Gandhi was the most perfect man, not including Christ, they all laughed. When I asked them why they laughed, they asked, 'What do you mean by perfect?' I said I don't mean he was perfect like a saint in the sense that he didn't move. I said he was perfect in the sense that he wasn't afraid to move and make things happen. And he didn't ask people to do things he couldn't do himself."[3]

Notes

1. Jacques Levy, *Cesar Chavez: Autobiography of La Causa* (New York: W. W. Norton & Company, 1975), p. 92.

2. Levy, *Cesar Chavez*, p. 92.

3. Levy, *Cesar Chavez*, p. 92.

CHAPTER ELEVEN

~

On Love

César Chávez observes in the following quotes that one of the most powerful aspects of his spirituality and one that he attempted to convey to others was that of love. Not romantic love but the love of one's fellow human beings. Here the role of Jesus no doubt inspired him. Jesus called on others to love not only God but also their neighbors, one of the Ten Commandments. César admitted that loving others, especially one's opponents, was not easy. Yet it was necessary to reinforce one's humanity.

***

"The force that is generated by that spirit of love is more powerful than any force on earth. It cannot be stopped."[1]

"[W]e need to remember that there was something which made that UNION, for unions are not pieces of merchandise to be bought at a corner store. Our union was born out of our common suffering, our common hopes for our children, and our common love for each other. Brothers and sisters, that love is still strong in our hearts. We think it is still strong in your hearts. We all must know that to let outsiders come in and destroy that love we have for each other is to destroy what we can make tomorrow mean for our children and our loved ones. We came as far as we are today through sticking together. We will go even further tomorrow if we remember that under everything else our strength is our love and respect for each other."[2]

"Let there be peace. Let there be justice. Let there be love. AMEN."[3]

"[T]rue wealth is not measured in money or status or power. It is measured by the legacy that we leave behind for those we love and those we inspire."[4]

"His dignity and worth as a man: these are very basic. He has to be able to do his work without being exploited. He has to be able to love."[5]

"Love is the most important ingredient in nonviolent work—love the opponent—but we really haven't learned yet how to love the growers. I think we've learned how not to hate them, and maybe love comes in stages. If we're full of hatred, we can't really do our work. Hatred saps all that strength and energy we need to plan. Of course, we can learn how to love the growers more easily after they sign contracts."[6]

Notes

1. John C. Hammerback and Richard J. Jensen, *The Rhetorical Career of César Chávez* (College Station: Texas A & M Press, 1998), p. 109.

2. Richard J. Jensen and John C. Hammerback, eds., *The Words of César Chávez* (College Station: Texas A & M Press, 2002), p. 79.

3. Hammerback and Jensen, *Rhetorical Career*, p. 135.

4. Hammerback and Jensen, *Rhetorical Career*, p. 152.

5. Frederick John Dalton, *The Moral Vision of César Chávez* (Maryknoll, NY: Orbis Books, 2003), p. 143.

6. Dalton, *Moral Vision*, p. 143.

César Chávez at Holman Methodist Church, Los Angeles, California, 1976. Nell Campbell.

~

CHAPTER TWELVE

On Truth

César Chávez believed that truth was on the side of the farm workers. It was the truth of the injustices that they faced. This truth was part of his spirituality in that César was of the opinion that this was also part of God's truth. God was on the side of the farm workers.

***

"Truth is on our side, even more than justice, because truth can't be changed. It has a way of manifesting itself. It has to come out, so sooner or later we'll win."[1]

"Truth is nonviolence. So everything really comes from truth. Truth is the ultimate. Truth is God."[2]

"Truth needs another element, and that is time. If you have those two elements, truth and time, and you understand them, then there is no reason why anyone would want to be violent. Number one, sooner or later truth is going to be exposed. It cannot be hidden, you know? Mankind has never been able to deal with the suppression of truth."[3]

Notes

1. Jacques Levy, *Cesar Chavez: Autobiography of La Causa.*(New York: W. W. Norton & Company, 1975), p. xviii.

2. Levy, *Cesar Chavez*, p. xviii.

3. Frederick John Dalton, *The Moral Vision of César Chávez* (Maryknoll, NY: Orbis Books, 2003), p. 142.

CHAPTER THIRTEEN

~

On Our Lady of Guadalupe

As part of his spirituality, César Chávez, like most people of Mexican descent, possessed a special devotion to Our Lady of Guadalupe. Since her believed appearance as the Mexican Mary, Mother of Jesus, in 1531 at Tepeyac on the outskirts of Mexico City, Mexicans on both sides of the border have embraced her as the patron saint of Mexico and of the Americas. For César, she was an image of the struggle of the Mexican people in history and among the farm workers for their liberation. Hence, she was a constant presence at the UFW's marches and demonstrations, as further noted in chapter 8.

***

[In April, 1959, César organized a march in the Mexican barrio of La Colonia in Oxnard to protest job discrimination among Mexican American workers as a result of the Bracero Program:]

"One of our ladies asked, 'Can I bring my banner of Our Lady of Guadalupe?' and I said, 'Yeah, sure. Bring her.' So I set her marching in front. That's where I got the idea that we needed some flag to identify us."[1]

Note

1. Jacques Levy, *Cesar Chavez: Autobiography of La Causa* (New York: W. W. Norton & Company, 1975), p. 140.

César Chávez on mountainside, 1988. Moises Sandoval/Courtesy of Maryknoll Fathers & Brothers.

CHAPTER FOURTEEN

~

On Prayer and Meditation

As part of his spirituality, César Chávez relied on prayer and meditation to refresh and renew his commitment to God, to his fellow human beings, to nonviolence, and to the cause for social justice. Besides attending daily mass, he prayed and meditated each day. At particular times, he took time off to do spiritual retreats, especially at Franciscan retreat houses. He shared a close affinity to the Franciscan way of life based on humility and sharing with others.

***

[During the 1970 lettuce strike, César took time to go on a spiritual retreat:]

"Besides being weak, I think that one of the reasons I went to the Franciscan retreat was because I wanted to plan strategy. I don't think I did this consciously, but that's what happened. It was a good place for me to be to meditate and pray. I was able to reflect on what was happening, to shed all of those million little problems, and to look at things a little more dispassionately."[1]

"Prayer is for you, for one's self. How do you reach somebody through prayer who does not give a hoot about what you are doing? But prayer reaches you. Your prayer then translates into action and determination and faith."[2]

[César on the Beatitudes, his favorite biblical passage:]
"[The Beatitudes] embody both charity and justice; and they speak directly to Christ's central message, which is 'Love thy neighbor.' We're doing Christ's work on earth; and we're reminded ever so much in the Beatitudes of what it is he wanted us to do: the thing about loving him and loving our neighbor.

"We're called on to be peacemakers at times, at times we're called to suffer persecution because of justice's sake, at times we deal with those who are poor in spirit, the meek, those who mourn, and especially those who hunger and thirst for justice. At times we have to be merciful as we do our work, and also we see in our work those who are clean of heart. So these Beatitudes are ever present in our work."[3]

"At these prayer meetings [during the grape strike], the workers got a chance to know the strikers. The foreman had spread vicious rumors about us, and this served to break down a lot of the suspicion and fears. I would say that the vigils we had were a decisive factor in winning the DiGiorgio campaign. The beautiful thing about it was this: The ideas came from the workers themselves. When you search out these ideas from among the people you can get out of almost any jam. This is the real meaning of nonviolence, as far as I'm concerned. Every day we had a mass, held a meeting, sang spirituals, and got them [the workers] to sign authorization cards. Those meetings were responsible in large part for keeping the spirit up of our people inside the camp and helping our organizing for the coming battle."[4]

["Prayer of the Farm Workers' Struggle"/"Oración del Campesino en la Lucha," written by César Chávez:]
"Show me the suffering of the most miserable;
So I will know my people's plight.
Free me to pray for others;
For you are present in every person.
Help me take responsibility for my own life;
So that I can be free at last.

Grant me the courage to serve others;
For in service there is true life.
Give me honesty and patience;
So that I can work with other workers.
Bring forth song and celebration;
So that the Spirit will be alive among us.
Let the Spirit flourish and grow;
So that we will never tire of the struggle.
Let us remember those who have died for justice;
For they have given us life.
Help us love even those who hate us;
So we can change the world.
Amen.[5]

Notes

1. Jacques Levy, *Cesar Chavez: Autobiography of La Causa* (New York: W. W. Norton & Company, 1975), p. 377.

2. Frederick John Dalton, *The Moral Vision of César Chávez* (Maryknoll, NY: Orbis Books, 2003), p. 137.

3. Dalton, *Moral Vision*, p. 162.

4. Dalton, *Moral Vision*, pp. 43–44.

5. Dalton, *Moral Vision*, pp. 155–156.

CHAPTER FIFTEEN

~

On the Spirituality of Antiracism

César Chávez, based on his own life experiences and his work with Mexican American farm workers, understood that part of the struggle had to do with confronting racism against people of Mexican descent. In his own life, he had faced the sting of racial discrimination. To combat racism, César developed what can be called a "spirituality of antiracism." This struggle became part of his overall spirituality aimed at achieving God's will that His people be treated with the dignity that they deserved as His children. Antiracism for César was not just a political issue, but a moral and spiritual one. As part of his opposition to racism, he, in very direct ways, scolded some Mexican Americans (Chicanos) for using racism themselves as they extolled the virtues of "La Raza." To César all human beings were equal.

***

[In elementary school in Arizona, Chavez initially encountered racial prejudice at hands of Anglo kids:]

"As tensions within the school increased, it was there that we first experienced discrimination and knew it. The first time it happened, it was a tiny incident, a chance remark, but one that I still remember. There were latrines in back of the school, and as I was returning from there, a couple of girls said something about 'dirty Mexicans.' I never forgot it. Words can be as painful as a switch, and many times those who say them are unaware how painful their words can be."[1]

[On segregated schools César attended in rural California:]

"And yet it was fortunate there was a lot of segregation then, because we got better treatment in segregated schools. We were not such oddballs. In integrated schools, where we were the only Mexicans, we were like monkeys in a cage. There were lots of racist remarks that still hurt my ears when I think of them."[2]

"Everywhere we went, to school, to the movies, there was this attack on our culture and our language, an attempt to make us conform to the 'American way.' What a sin!"[3]

"That dream [of ending racism against farm workers] grew from my own experience with racism, with hope, with the desire to be treated fairly and to see my people treated as human beings, not as chattel.

"It grew from anger and rage, emotions I felt forty and fifty years ago when people my color were denied the right to see a movie or eat at a restaurant in many parts of California. It grew from the frustration and humiliation I felt as a boy who couldn't understand how the growers could abuse and exploit farm workers when there were so many of us and so few of them.

"Later, in the 1950s, I began to realize what other minority people had discovered: The only answer, the only hope, was in organizing. All Latinos, urban and rural, young and old, are connected to the farm workers' experience. We all lived through the fields, or our parents did. We shared that common humiliation."[4]

[César recalled how one grower treated Mexican farm workers:]

"At different times he talked about those 'niggers' in the fields and he called the Mexicans 'my boys.'

"I finally shook my head and said, 'That's all. No more!' I told him, 'These are grown men. Why do you keep calling them boys?'

"He couldn't understand what was wrong. 'Well, I've always called them that, and they don't mind, so why should you care?'

"Even if it's all right with you and your men, it's not all right with the Union. So we will no longer call them boys or 'niggers.' It was the same education we seem to go through with everybody."[5]

[Commenting at a congressional hearing held in Delano in the early months of the grape strike:]
"Hearings similar to these have been called for decades, and unfortunately things have not changed very much in spite of them. The same labor camps which were used 30 years ago at the time of the La Follette committee hearings [1930s] are still housing our workers. The same exploitation of child labor, the same idea that farm workers are a different breed of people—humble, happy, built close to the ground—prevails."[6]

"[W]e oppose some of this La Raza business so much. We know what it does. When La Raza means or implies racism, we don't support it. But if it means our struggle, our dignity, or our cultural roots, then we're for it. I guess many times people don't know what they mean by La Raza, but we can't be against racism on the one hand and for it on the other."[7]

"La Raza? Why be racist. Our belief is to help everyone, not just one race. Humanity is our belief."[8]

"Growers don't want to lose power over the people. It is a mixed-up kind of paternalism. They are very paternalistic but they don't know our people. . . . They just don't comprehend our life, our dignity, our values. Their mentality is something like that you find in the white southern racist. He feels that if he accepts the black he loses his manhood somehow. The growers feel the same way about us."[9]

[César on the California Farm Bureau, the representative of the growers:]
"Because of their extreme racist attitude they have made our union their primary target because they cannot deal with unions made up of minority groups and led by minorities."[10]

"When the racists and bigots, the industrialists and the corporation farmers were not shedding our blood, they were blocking our way with all kinds of stratagems. We have heard them all—'Property Rights,' 'States Rights,' 'Right to Work.' All of these slogans . . . have been uttered in ringing tones of idealism and individual freedom. But that is the special genius of those who would deny the right of others and hoard the fruits of democracy for themselves: They evade the problems and complex challenges of equal justice by reducing them to primitive oversimplifications that plead for nothing else but the perpetuation of their own special, exploitative interests."[11]

[On the killing of Nagi Daifallah, a farm worker, in 1973 by a Kern County sheriff deputy:]

"Nagi Daifallah is dead at the age of 24. The hand that struck Brother Nagi down trembles in fear. It too is the victim of the climate of violence, racism, and hatred created by those men who own everything . . . and kill what they cannot own.

"We are faced with discrimination, exploitation, and even slaughter. The government represses our people and millions of farm workers are trapped in poverty while the growers lavish in the riches we have earned for them.

"These are differing ills, but they are the common works of greedy men. They reflect the imperfections of society.

"In the struggle to change these evils, Nagi gave his life."[12]

Notes

1. Jacques Levy, *Cesar Chavez: Autobiography of La Causa* (New York: W. W. Norton & Company,1975), pp. 29–30.

2. Frederick John Dalton, *The Moral Vision of César Chávez* (Maryknoll, NY: Orbis Books, 2003), p. 13.

3. Dalton, *Moral Vision*, p. 13.

4. Dalton, *Moral Vision*, pp. 65–66.

5. Dalton, *Moral Vision*, p. 66.

6. Dalton, *Moral Vision*, p. 66.

7. Levy, *Cesar Chavez*, p. 123.

8. Richard Griswold del Castillo and Richard A. García, *César Chávez: A Triumph of Spirit* (Norman: University of Oklahoma Press, 1995), p. 154.

9. Dalton, *Moral Vision*, p. 67.

10. Dalton, *Moral Vision*, p. 67.

11. Dalton, *Moral Vision*, pp. 67–68.

12. Dalton, *Moral Vision*, p. 107.

~

CHAPTER SIXTEEN

On Ecumenism and Brotherhood

There is no question but that one of the strengths of César Chávez's leadership concerned his ability to reach out and construct alliances across ethnic, class, and religious lines. Although a Catholic, César, for example, believed in ecumenism and brotherhood with people of other faiths. As a result, many Protestant and Jewish denominations and individuals rallied to support the farm workers' cause. Indeed, César often chided his own Church about trailing behind other religious groups in endorsing the initial grape strike.

***

[In the1950s, the Community Service Organization sent César to organize in Madera, California. There he met a Pentecostal preacher who came to César because he wanted help on his immigration status. He invited César to his home, where he excused himself to conduct a service and went to his living room that served as his church:]

"After they started their service, I asked if I could join them. In those days there was a lot of separation between Protestants and Catholics; in San Jose I was one of the few Catholics who attended Protestant services. When we first came to *Sal Si Puedes* [the San Jose barrio], Protestants were the ones who gave us lodging and food and invited my mother to the services. She wasn't afraid of them. So in that little Madera church, I observed everything going on about me that could be useful in organizing. Although there were no more than twelve men and women, there was more spirit there than when I went to a mass where there were two hundred. Everybody was happy. They all were singing. These people were really committed in their beliefs, and this made them sing and clap and participate. I liked that."[1]

"If we were nothing but farm workers in the Union now, just Mexican farm workers, we'd have about 30 percent of all the ideas we have. There would be no cross-fertilization, no growing. It's beautiful to work with other groups, other ideas and other customs. It's like the wood is laminated."[2]

"I think that our philosophy of cooperation with all groups has helped us a great deal. Our people have developed the ability to respect every one with whom they came into contact."[3]

[Letter to National Council of Churches, February 20, 1968:]
"Our struggle in Delano is not over. In some ways it becomes more difficult each day. Our success (or failure) here and the quality of the organization we build will help us to shape the future for farm workers everywhere in our country. We do not take this responsibility lightly. But we cannot be faithful to this responsibility without the participation of the Christian community. You can help us to survive and win new victories; but because of who you represent you can also help us stay true to our intention to serve our fellow farm workers."[4]

Notes

1. Jacques Levy, *Cesar Chavez: Autobiography of La Causa* (New York: W. W. Norton & Company, 1975), pp. 115–116.

2. Richard Griswold del Castillo and Richard A. García, *César Chávez: A Triumph of Spirit* (Norman: University of Oklahoma Press, 1995), p. 48.

3. Griswold del Castillo and García, *César Chávez*, p. 99.

4. Winthrop Yinger, *Cesar Chavez: The Rhetoric of Nonviolence* (Hicksville, NY: Exposition Press, 1975), pp. 108–109.

Makeshift altar at César Chávez's funeral in 1993. Mario T. García.

CHAPTER SEVENTEEN

~

On Humility, the Spirituality of Nondiscrimination, and Death

Finally, these last quotes relate to the humility of César Chávez that so many people observed. Although a man of great stature and influence, he remained modest in his daily life and as humble as the farm workers he served. He was also a man who did not believe in discriminating between people of different ethnic backgrounds and as such developed what can be considered a "spirituality of nondiscrimination." In addition, perhaps in anticipation of his own eventual death, César commented on the importance of recognizing the inevitability of death not in order to fear it, but to accept it. By accepting death, you prepared for it and attempted to live your life, as he did, by knowing that you had served in life both God and man. César Chávez accomplished this and, to slightly paraphrase his own words, "died rightly."

***

"[I]n defeat there must be courage. But . . . in victory there must be humility."[1]

[In the early days of the grape strike, César reacted to criticism of welcoming Anglos and other volunteers and to having alliances with them:]

139

"On discrimination we spoke up right away, 'Black people, brown people, they're all part of the Union,' we said. 'If you don't like it, then get out, but we're not going to change it.' I've been discriminated against, and it's a very horrible feeling. You can't do anything back. Of course, discrimination is bad for all the moral reasons, but it is also bad for reasons of unity. It can quickly destroy the Movement."[2]

"To be hungry and thirsty also included a primitive passion for food and water that had to do with survival itself. To be hungry and thirsty was a part of life but it was also a reminder of death. In a very real way it was a manner of life and death."[3]

"Death comes to us all and we do not get to choose the time or the circumstances of our dying. The hardest thing of all is to die rightly."[4]

Notes

1. John C. Hammerback and Richard J. Jensen, *The Rhetorical Career of César Chávez* (College Station: Texas A & M Press, 1998), p. 99.
2. Jacques Levy, *Cesar Chavez: Autobiography of La Causa* (New York: W. W. Norton & Company, 1975), p. 198.
3. *National Catholic Reporter*, March 7, 1975.
4. Richard J. Jensen and John C. Hammerback, eds., *The Words of César Chávez* (College Station: Texas A & M Press, 2002), pp. 172–173.

~

Selected Bibliography

Backus, Berthat Rhodes, "A Communicator for 'La Causa': A Burkean Analysis of the Rhetoric of César Chávez," Ph.D. disseration, University of California, Santa Barbara, 1970.

"Cesar Chavez Looks Back on Long Struggle," *Imperial Valley News*, April 25, 1972, in Anne Loftis Collection, Box 8, Fld. 2 in Special Collections, Green Library, Stanford University.

César Chávez to Dear Sister and Brother, March 10, 1970 in Anne Draper Collection, Box 4, Fld. 2 in Special Collections, Green Library, Stanford University.

Chávez, César, "Creative Non-Violence," *The Center Magazine*, vol. 2, no. 2 (March 1969).

Chávez, César, "The Mexican-American and the Church," in F. Chris García, ed., *La Causa Politica: A Chicano Political Reader*. Notre Dame: University of Notre Dame Press, 1974, p. 143; first published in *El Grito*, vol. 1, no. 4 (Summer 1968), pp. 9–12.

Dalton, Frederick John, *The Moral Vision of César Chávez*. Maryknoll, NY: Orbis Books, 2003.

Day, Mark, *Forty Acres: Cesar Chavez and the Farm Workers*. New York: Praeger Publishers, 1971.

Ferriss, Susan, and Ricardo Sandoval, *The Fight in the Fields: Cesar Chavez and the Farmworkers Movement*. New York: Harcourt Brace & Company, 1997.

Fitch, Bob, "Tilting with the System: An Interview with Cesar Chavez," in Chris García, ed., *Chicano Politics: Readings*. New York: MSS Information Corp., 1973, pp. 174–182. Originally published in *The Christian Century* (February 10, 1970).

Goodwin, David, *Cesar Chavez: Hope for the People*. New York: Fawcett Columbine, 1991.

Griswold del Castillo, Richard, and Richard A. García, *César Chávez: Triumph of Spirit*. Norman: University of Oklahoma Press, 1995.

Hammerback, John C., and Richard J. Jensen, *The Rhetorical Career of César Chávez*. College Station: Texas A & M Press, 1998.

Hammerback, John C., and Richard J. Jensen, eds., *The Words of César Chávez*. College Station: Texas A & M Press, 2002.

Hammerback, John C., Richard J. Jensen, and José Angel Gutiérrez, *A War of Words: Chicano Protest in the 1960s and 1970s*. Westport, CT: Greenwood Press, 1985.

Hoffman, Pat, *Ministry of the Dispossessed: Learning from the Farm Worker Movement*. Los Angeles: Wallace Press, 1987.

Levy, Jacques, *Cesar Chavez: Autobiography of La Causa*. New York: W. W. Norton & Company, 1975.

López y Rivas, Gilberto, ed., *The Chicano: Life and Struggles of the Mexican Minority in the United States*. New York: Monthly Review Press, 1973.

"El Malcriado: The Voice of the Farm Worker," in Luis Valdez and Stan Steiner, eds., *Aztlan: An Anthology of Mexican American Literature*. New York: Alfred A. Knopf, 1972, p. 208.

"March of the Migrants," *Life*, April 29, 1966, pp. 93–94.

Matthiessen, Peter, *Sal Si Puedes: Cesar Chavez and the New American Revolution*. New York: Random House, 1969.

Moyer, John R., "A Conversation with César Chávez," in Meier and Rivera, *Readings on La Raza: The Twentieth Century*. New York: Hill and Wang, 1979. First published in John R. Moyer, "A Conversation with César Chávez," in *Journal of Current Social Issues*, vol. 9, no. 3 (November–December 1970).

"Plan de Delano," in Gilberto López y Rivas, ed., *The Chicano: Life and Struggles of the Mexican Minority in the United States*. New York: Monthly Review Press, 1973.

Solis-Garza, Luis A., "César Chávez: The Chicano 'Messiah?'" in Edward Simmen, *In Pain and Promise: The Chicano Today* (New York: New American Library, 1972).

"Statement by César Chávez read by Rev. James Drake to nearly 8,000 farm workers, March 10, 1968 at the conclusion of a 25 day Fast for Non-Violence," as printed in Berthat Rhodes Backus, "A Communicator for 'La Causa': A Burkeian Analysis of the Rhetoric of César Chávez," Ph.D. dissertation, University of California, Santa Barbara, 1970, p. 99.

Taylor, Ronald B., *Chavez and the Farm Workers*. Boston: Beacon Press, 1975.

Valdez, Luis, and Stan Steiner, eds., *Aztlan: An Anthology of Mexican American Literature* (New York: Vintage Books, 1972).

Yett, Jane Marie, "Farm Labor Struggles in California, 1970–1973, In Light of Reinhold Niebuhr's Concepts of Power and Justice," unpublished Ph.D. dissertation, Graduate Theological Union, Berkeley, 1980.

Yinger, Winthrop, *Cesar Chavez: The Rhetoric of Nonviolence*. Hicksville, NY: Exposition Press, 1975.

César Chávez with Mario T. García and his children, Giuliana (left) and Carlo. Casa de la Raza, Santa Barbara, California, 1990. Mario T. García.

~

About the Editor

Mario T. García is professor of history and Chicano studies at the University of California, Santa Barbara. The son of a Mexican immigrant and a U.S.-born Mexican American, Dr. García grew up in the border town of El Paso, Texas. He is the author of several books on Mexican American history and Chicano Catholic history, including *Desert Immigrants: The Mexicans of El Paso, 1880-1920; Mexican Americans: Leadership, Ideology & Identity, 1930-1960;* and *Memories of Chicano History: The Life and Narrative of Bert Corona.* Several of his books have been honored with a Southwest Book Award, and he has been the recipient of distinguished fellowships such as a Guggenheim Fellowship and a Woodrow Wilson Center Fellowship.